Book & Lyrics by
Vin Morreale, Jr.

Music by
Eric B. Sirota

academyartspress.com

ISBN: 978-1-0880-1309-0

You can hear a fully produced radio version of *A DAY AT THE WHITE HOUSE: The Sparx Brothers Go To Washington* at both *academyarts.com* and *whitehouseplay.com.*

CAST

Principals: 2F, 10M (Doubling Possible)
Chorus: 5-10 Singers, M or F

JESSICA WOODARD	38, Highly Professional
JORDAN FLETCHER	40, Idealistic, Reserved
THE SPARX BROTHERS CRENHAW SPARX CHEATO SPARX HOBO SPARX	30-50, Zany Con Artists
THE THREE STUPIDS BARRY BO CURBEY	28-60, The Joint Chiefs
CABOT & ODDFELLOW JUDD CABOT LOU ODDFELLOW	28-60, State Dept. Staff
MAE WAIST	34, Seductive Lobbyist
W.Z. FIELDING	55, EPA Chief

SENATORS, REPORTERS & COMEDIAN CHORUS

SETTING

ACT I	Outside the White House & The Oval Office
ACT II	The Oval Office
EPILOGUE	Outside the White House

SONGS

ACT ONE

ACT TWO

EPILOGUE

FOR BAND REQUIREMENTS & LINKS TO SONG RECORDINGS, PLEASE CONTACT ERIC@ERICSIROTA.COM

ACT ONE

AT RISE: The curtain rises to reveal a painted backdrop of the White House exterior and grounds. Throughout the opening number, various groups of people will enter - TOURISTS, TV CREWS, REPORTERS, BUREAUCRATS, POLITICIANS, LOBBYISTS. The atmosphere is charged with anticipation.

"A CHANGE IN THE WHTE HOUSE"

GATHERING CROWD. *(Singing)*

HAVE YOU HEARD,
SPREAD THE WORD.

HAVE YOU HEARD
THE EXCITEMENT IS GROWING
SPREAD THE WORD
THERE'S A NEW WIND BLOWING
A NEW FACE IN TOWN
HISTORY IS MADE TODAY
THERE'S A CHANGE IN THE WHITE HOUSE
A NEW LEADER OF THE USA

HE'S THE ONE
WHO CHARMED THE NATION
TODAY IS HIS INAUGURATION
A NEW SENSE OF HOPE
SURE TO BE A BRIGHTER DAY
THERE'S A CHANGE IN THE WHITE HOUSE
A NEW LEADER OF THE USA

MORE

GATHERING CROWD. *(Singing)*

HE SAYS HE
WILL KEEP HIS PROMISES
HE'LL SHOW ALL
THE DOUBTING THOMASES
THE PEOPLE HAVE SPOKEN
DEMOCRACY HAS HAD ITS SAY
THERE'S A CHANGE IN THE WHITE HOUSE
A NEW LEADER OF THE USA

NEWS MEDIA. *(Singing)*

HE'S JUST ONE
MORE POLITICIAN
WE'LL REPORT
WITH SUSPICION
A QUICK HONEYMOON
THEN BACK TO GRIDLOCK EACH AND EVERY DAY
THERE'S A CHANGE IN THE WHITE HOUSE
A NEW LEADER OF THE USA

SENATORS. *(Singing)*

ON THE HILL
WE RESPECT HIS STATION
BUT WE'RE THE ONES
WHO MAKE LEGISLATION
WE'LL TAKE HIS SIDE
WHEN HE DOES EXACTLY WHAT WE SAY
FORGET ABOUT THE WHITE HOUSE
WE'RE THE LEADERS OF THE USA

(The mood suddenly shifts. The next verse is soft, almost reverential.)

ALL. *(Singing)*

A YEAR FROM NOW
WE'LL START TO GRUMBLE
AS HIS POLLS
BEGIN TO TUMBLE
WE'LL HOLD OUT HOPE
FOR THE NEXT ELECTION DAY
ANOTHER CHANGE IN THE WHITE HOUSE
WITH A NEW LEADER OF THE USA

WE'LL MAKE A CHANGE IN THE WHITE HOUSE
A CHANGE IN THE WHITE HOUSE
A CHANGE IN THE WHITE HOUSE
A NEW LEADER OF THE USA!

(The crowd disperses, murmuring with excitement. As we move into the White House and the OVAL OFFICE. Presidential portraits hang on the wall, Washington, Lincoln, Jefferson. A large desk with telephone and scattered papers occupies UpStage Center. An American flag stands UpStage Left. Doors Stage Left and Right provide access. Two ornate chairs are placed on either side of the room. A large sofa occupies the Downstage Left area. JORDEN FLETCHER (40, highly professional yet idealistic) is sprawled on the sofa. As White House Chief of Protocol, Jorden is well-groomed and exceptionally well-mannered. But at the moment, his jaw hangs open as he snores.

JESSICA. *(OFFSTAGE)* Jorden! Jorden Fletcher!

JORDEN. *(Waking)* Huh... Wha..?

(JESSICA WOODARD (30s, attractive, with a warm, yet business-like manner.) enters DR. As White House Press Secretary, she maintains an aggressive, no-nonsense posture.

JESSICA. Jorden! What are you doing?! He'll be here any minute!

JORDEN. Sorry... uh, I must have drifted off...

JESSICA. How can you sleep at a time like this?! The newly elected President of the United States' first visit to the Oval Office, and his Chief of Protocol schedules an appointment in La La Land!

JORDEN. *(Leaping up.)* I don't know what happened, Jessica! It must have been the whole Inauguration thing. It's not easy coordinating the transition for an incoming President.

(Together they begin frantically straightening up the Oval Office. They find golf clubs under the sofa, an old shoe, a pair of pantyhose, a framed picture of Martin Van Buren with a mustache drawn on it, an old cigar, a half-chewed pretzel, and other unexpected items.

JESSICA. I don't want to hear it, Fletcher. You haven't been working any harder than I have. And you don't see me taking naps!

JORDEN. That's because you're Wonder Woman. Jessica Woodard - Mistress of efficiency. The sparkling radiance that lights up the Potomac...

JESSICA. *(Not harshly.)* With that ballet of bull, you should be Press Secretary, instead of me.

JORDEN. And face those piranha in the press corps? Not on your life. You keep the cameras and the glory. I'll sit in the shadows and make sure the White House runs smoothly. Think of me as the country's First House-Husband.

JESSICA. Well, hubby, you better be ready to do your job, because I hear this new President's a handful.

JORDEN. They all are. But think of it, Jessica. Here we are. In the White House. Standing on the cusp of history…

"THIS IS WHERE IT STARTS"

JORDEN. (Singing)

THIS IS WHERE IT STARTS
ALL THAT I HAVE DREAMED OF
FOLLOWING MY HEART
AT LAST, I AM HERE
TIME TO PLAY MY PART
FOR THE NATION I LOVE
MY MOMENT HAS ARRIVED
CAN'T WAIT ANOTHER YEAR

ALL MY LIFE HAS POINTED TO
THIS PLACE THAT WE ARE NOW
IN WASHINGTON, WHERE NOBLE SOULS
PROTECT THE LIVES OF ALL

WITH VIRTUE WISE
THESE SELFLESS GALS AND GUYS
SAFEGUARD THE CONSTITUTION
AND THANKS TO FATE
I JOIN THIS GREAT
AND LOFTY INSTITUTION

ALL MY LIFE HAS POINTED TO
THIS PLACE THAT WE ARE NOW
IN WASHINGTON, WHERE NOBLE SOULS
PROTECT THE LIVES OF ALL

MORE

JORDEN. (Singing)

THIS IS WHERE IT STARTS
ALL THAT I HAVE WORKED FOR
ALL THAT I BELIEVE
AND NOW MY CHOICE IS CLEAR
A BRAND NEW PRESIDENT
A CHANCE TO MAKE A DIFFERENCE
FOR POSTERITY
AND ALL THAT I HOLD DEAR

THIS IS WHERE IT STARTS
I PRAY THAT I AM WORTHY
BUT WITH YOU BY MY SIDE
MY DREAMS WILL ALL COME TRUE

JORDEN and JESSICA. (Singing)
SHARING THEM WITH YOU
IS ALL I WANT TO DO

JESSICA. After all this time, you still believe that? Like Washington is some kind of Eden of Ethics, and you get to usher them into the garden?

JORDEN. It's why I'm here. To make a difference.

JESSICA. God, you're such a boy scout.

JORDEN. Guilty as charged.

JESSICA. Well, I hope you win your optimism badge, because it sounds like our new President is on his way.

(A few bars of "Hail To The Chief" waft in from offstage, accompanied by the sound of a swelling cheer. We can barely make out the President's voice saying "Thank you. Thank You..." above the din of the crowd. Jorden and Jessica toss the last of the odd items under the sofa, as the Stage Left door opens and CRENSHAW SPARX (who bears an uncanny resemblance to Groucho Marx, with cigar, coattails, painted mustache and irreverent attitude) bursts in.)

CRENSHAW. Geesh. The way they were cheering, you'd think my fly was open. It's not, is it?

JORDEN. Uh, no, sir.

CRENSHAW. Well, remind me to consider that when my popularity begins to sag. Of course, at my age, everything begins to sag. (aside) I can see a few people in the audience know what I'm talking about... I'm talking to you in the third row. (to Jorden & Jessica) So who are you? Groupies or gropies? I have little patience for groupies, but I do enjoy a little gropie now and then.

JORDEN. I am Jorden Fletcher. White House Chief of Protocol. And you already know Jessica Woodard, your Press Secretary. She is your voice to the public.

CRENSHAW. I thought that's what Twitter was for?

JORDEN & JESSICA. *(Together.)* No! Not Twitter!!

CRENSHAW. That's right. We probably don't need another Twitterer-In-Chief. *(Ogles Jessica.)* Press Secretary, huh? You're the one who makes the country believe I know what I'm talking about?

JESSICA. I'll try my best, sir.

CRENSHAW. Well, don't do too good of a job of it. I'd hate to break a long-standing Presidential tradition. I'm President Sparx. But you can call me Crenshaw, Crenshaw Sparx. Or you can call me Mr. President. Chief Executive of the United States. The living Symbol of Democracy. Leader of the Free World. (aside) This is gonna look great on my resume! (to Jorden) Aren't you going to kiss my ring?

JORDEN. Uh...you're not wearing one, sir?

CRENSHAW. Then kiss my earring. No, better yet, let her do that. You look like a nibbler.

(He grabs Jessica and dips her backwards passionately. She is too surprised to object.)

CRENSHAW. *(CONT'D)* Ah, Miss Woodard, has anyone ever told you your eyes are like two lurid pools of fluoridated water?

JESSICA. No... but...

CRENSHAW. Has anyone ever told you your eyes are like two bright sapphires in a sea of white chocolate?

JESSICA. Mr. President...

CRENSHAW. How about two pitted olives in a martini glass?

JESSICA. Mr. President, please...

CRENSHAW. People don't talk to you much, do they?

JORDEN. Sir, as Chief of Protocol, I must remind you of the many federal laws against sexual harassment.

CRENSHAW. Listen, Fletcher. Nobody knows more about sexual harassment than me...except all seven of my court-appointed attorneys, that is.

(He suddenly spins Jessica into an upright position and steps away.)

JESSICA. Mr. President! I am a career political spokesperson. I have spent fourteen years working my way up to this position. I have earned a certain degree of respect!

CRENSHAW. I couldn't agree more! Fletcher, behave yourself!

JORDEN. *(Incredulous.)* Behave myself, sir?

CRENSHAW. If you do, I may not have to.

JESSICA. Mr. President, this is hardly the best way to begin a working relationship.

CRENSHAW. You're right, Miss Woodard. Forgive my tiny hands. My behavior was rude and inappropriate. Stick out your arms.

(Confused by his odd, rapid-fire requests, she holds her hands out. He falls backwards into her arms, so she is now dipping him.)

CRENSHAW. *(CONT'D)* Now it's your turn to be inappropriate for a while.

JESSICA. Mr. President! Control yourself!

CRENSHAW. *(Jumping up.)* If I could control myself, what kind of politician would I be? What would the folks on Capitol Hill think? The folks on Capitol Hill do think, don't they?

JORDEN. *(Dryly)* There's a rumor to that effect, sir.

(Crenshaw begins pacing the room, in classic Marx Brother style.)

CRENSHAW. So why do they call this place the Oval Office?

JESSICA. Because of its shape, Mr. President.

CRENSHAW. You mean, because it's round?

JESSICA. Elliptical, sir.

CRENSHAW. What?

JESSICA. Elliptical.

CRENSHAW. Thanks, but I'm not in the mood for a 'lip tickle' right now. But when I am, I'll be sure to let you know. Now that you mention it, this room really isn't that round.

JESSICA. No, sir. It's elliptical.

CRENSHAW. You're doing it again.

JESSICA. I'm sorry, sir.

CRENSHAW. It's more like a circle with low self-esteem. Either that or I don't know my Algebra.

JORDEN. Geometry.

CRENSHAW. What?

JORDEN. Geometry.

CRENSHAW. You sure don't look like one.

JORDEN. Like what, sir?

CRENSHAW. A tree... But this is the executive branch, so you never know.

JORDEN. I didn't say "Gee, I'm a tree." I said "Geometry."

CRENSHAW. Well, Gee, I'm a bush. No, wait. We already had a couple of those in this office already.

JORDEN. *(Exasperated)* Will there be anything else, sir?

CRENSHAW. Is the hot line to the Soviet Union still hooked up?

JORDEN. Russia, sir.

CRENSHAW. Gesundheit.

JORDEN. Sir?

CRENSHAW. The hot line. Where is it?

JORDEN. Just press line three on your telephone, Mr. President.

CRENSHAW. Line three is the hot line?

JORDEN. That's correct.

CRENSHAW. Is anything else in this room hot? I'm pretty sure there will be before I'm through. Thank you, Mr. Fletcher. Miss Woodard. That will be all.

JESSICA. Very good, sir.

CRENSHAW. I'd rather not be. But no time for that. I have a call to make.

(Jessica and Jorden exit Stage Right, glad to be leaving this lunatic. As soon as the door closes behind them, Crenshaw scampers behind the desk.)

CRENSHAW. *(CONT'D)* Let's see. Line three.

(He grabs the telephone and pushes the button. Suddenly, he drops the receiver and waves his hand in pain.)

CRENSHAW. *(CONT'D)* Yow! Hot line!

(He pulls a handkerchief from his pocket and wraps it around the receiver. As he waits for someone to pick up, he rifles through the desk, shoving heirlooms in his pocket.)

CRENSHAW. *(Into phone.)* Oh, Hello! I'm looking for Lenin. Fine Lenin. Although something in a nice percale might do... Vladimir Lenin? Well, I don't know. Do you think it would go with my pillowcases? *(To audience.)* I've always wanted to do this. *(Into phone.)* Stop talking foreign. It's un-American. I don't care what you are, do you have Lenin or not? What? He's dead? Lenin's dead? Does Yoko Ono know? Yoko. Yoko... The yellow thing in the middle of an Italian egg. What? Well, Chechnya to you, too! *(Slams the phone down.)* Some hot line. Bet you can't even get late night singles lines on it...

(The Stage Right door flies open, as CHEATO and HOBO SPARX fall into the room. They look and act like Chico and Harpo Marx. They both press their ears to the door to see if they're being followed. After a beat, they relax.)

CHEATO. Ya'see? I told you thosa Secret Service guys have no sensa humor.

(Hobo slaps his leg, pantomimes pulling an Agent's pants down, then tries to imitate how difficult it would be to chase someone with your pants around your ankles. He and Cheato laugh hysterically, although Hobo's laugh is also silent.)

CHEATO. *(CONT'D)* I guess it'sa no secret where he keep his service revolver, eh?

CRENSHAW. Excuse me. Mind if I ask who you are?

CHEATO. No, I no mind. *(To Hobo)* You mind if he ask who we are? *(Hobo shrugs.)* No. He no mind either.

CRENSHAW. I'm glad to hear it.

(Long pause. They all wait, trying too hard to act casual. After a long beat.)

CRENSHAW. *(CONT'D)* So... who are you?

CHEATO. That-a depends. You a cop?

CRENSHAW. No.

CHEATO. FBI?

CRENSHAW. Not really.

CHEATO. CIA?

CRENSHAW. Not that I know of.

CHEATO. NSA?

CRENSHAW. Don't think so.

CHEATO. ASPCA

CRENSHAW. Can't say that I am.

CHEATO. L-M-N-O-P?

CRENSHAW. Not the last time I checked.

CHEATO. Then who are you?

CRENSHAW. I'm the new President.

CHEATO. Oh, The President. *(To Hobo.)* Hey, Hobo! Thisa the guy who choppa'd down the cherry tree...

CRENSHAW. No. That was President Washington.

CHEATO. Oh. Then you musta be the guy who choppa'd down slavery.

CRENSHAW. That was Lincoln.

CHEATO. The guy who choppa'd the tax rates?

CRENSHAW. President Reagan.

CHEATO. Oh. Then you musta be the guy who likes pork chops.

CRENSHAW. That's the one. Just think. I'm in office one day, and already my administration is being remembered for something historic. Now that we've got that settled...Who are you?

CHEATO. I'ma Vito Pasquale McConnell. Senate Majority Leader.

CRENSHAW. Oh? And what's your majority?

CHEATO. Liberal Arts. But I'ma thinkin'a majorityng in Poly Sci next semester.

HOBO. *(Honking his bicycle horn.)* Honk.

CRENSHAW. And who's he?

CHEATO. He'sa the Speaker of the House.

HOBO. *(Honking his bicycle horn.)* Honk.

CRENSHAW. The Speaker of The House?

CHEATO. That'sa right.

HOBO. *(Honking his bicycle horn.)* Honk.

CRENSHAW. Does he talk?

CHEATO. No.

CRENSHAW. But he's Speaker of the House?

CHEATO. They don' have a lot to say downa there.

HOBO. *(Honking his bicycle horn.)* Honk.

CRENSHAW. Well, does he pass legislation?

CHEATO. No. But he ate a lotta oat bran yesterday and he's been passing digestation all day long.

CRENSHAW. I know.

CHEATO. How you know?

CRENSHAW. I got wind of it. So tell me, Senator...uh Vito...are you a Republican or a Democrat?

CHEATO. Which isa which?

CRENSHAW. Republicans are the elephants and Democrats are the donkeys.

CHEATO. So that'sa why there's so many overweight jackasses in Congress!

CRENSHAW. Let me put it another way. The Democrats want to raise your taxes and give everything you make to the poor...until they make everyone in the country too poor to pay taxes, so they can then qualify for handouts from the Democrats.

CHEATO. And whadda they do when they run outta money?

CRENSHAW. They blame the Republicans.

CHEATO. Hokay. And what do the Republicans do?

CRENSHAW. The Republicans back a budget with tax breaks for big business, until the business of big breaks breaks the back of the budget... conservatively speaking.

CHEATO. And whadda they do when they run outta money?

CRENSHAW. They blame the Democrats.

HOBO. *(Honking his bicycle horn.)* Honk.

CHEATO. He says he still no gets how alla this works.

CRENSHAW. Let me try to explain...

"OBFUSCATION"

CRENSHAW. (Singing)

A LITTLE POLITICS
A BIT OF THAT AND THIS
A LITTLE SLIGHT OF HAND
TO COVER WHAT'S AMISS

CUE THE SMOKE AND MIRRORS
FLASH THE SHINY LIGHTS
BEFORE THEY KNOW WHAT HIT 'EM,
YOU CAN TAKE AWAY THEIR RIGHTS

IT'S ALL AN ILLUSION
A MAGIC TRICK, YOU SEE
BUT IF YOU SEE, IT'S UP TO ME
TO CONFUSE YOU TOTALLY

MORE

CRENSHAW. (Singing)

OB-FU-SCA-TION!
CONSTERNATION
IT ALL COMES DOWN TO THIS
DEDICATION
TO PREVARICATION
THEIR WORDS ARE MEANINGLESS
ALL THEIR WORDS ARE MEANINGLESS

A LITTLE JINGOISM
A SOUNDBITE TO REPEAT
IF YOU SAY JUST WHAT YOU MEAN,
THEY'LL LABEL YOU A CHEAT

DANCE AROUND THE ISSUES
MUDDY UP THE FACTS
AND IF YOU'RE CAUGHT THE BEST DEFENSE
IS AN UNPROVOKED ATTACK

OB-FU-SCA-TION!
CONSTERNATION
IT ALL COMES DOWN TO THIS
DEDICATION
TO PREVARICATION
THEIR WORDS ARE MEANINGLESS
ALL THEIR WORDS ARE MEANINGLESS

CONSIDER THIS A PRIMER
ON POLITICAL DECEIT
LYING HAS ITS OWN REWARD
THE HONEST KNOW DEFEAT
LET THE HONEST KNOW DEFEAT!

CRENSHAW. So which are you, a Democrat or a Republican?

CHEATO. Which one isa the donkey?

CRENSHAW. The Democrats.

CHEATO. Then I'm a co-dependent.

CRENSHAW. You mean Independent.

CHEATO. No. I'ma co-dependent. You gotta be to make any sense outta this Congress thing.

CRENSHAW. What about the Speaker?

HOBO. *(Honking his bicycle horn.)* Honk.

CHEATO. He's a Whig.

CRENSHAW. Don't be silly. The Whig party hasn't been around since the American Revolution.

CHEATO. Then he's a toupee.

CRENSHAW. That explains it. I was afraid he got a hair transplant from an electrocuted sheep.

CHEATO. Don't insult his hair. He's very sensitive about his roots. They used to call him carrot-top.

(Hobo pulls a small carrot out of his hair and begins to eat it.)

CRENSHAW. What do they call him now?

HOBO. *(Honking his bicycle horn.)* Honk.

CRENSHAW. Well, I'm glad that was censored.

CHEATO. So now you know alla 'bout us. What about you?

CRENSHAW. Little old me? I'm just another pretty face.

CHEATO. Boy, do they need a mirror ina this place! So, how come-a you get to be President?

CRENSHAW. Well, last election, the Republicans and the Democrats were neck and neck. And since my neck was longer, I won.

CHEATO. Serves them right for necking in public. How many votes you get?

CRENSHAW. Nine.

CHEATO. Nine?

CRENSHAW. Six Supreme Court justices... and three coeds in Berkeley who thought they were voting for Karl Marx.

CHEATO. Karla Marx? Who'sa that?

CRENSHAW. He wrote the Communist Manifesto.

CHEATO. Oh sure! I made Manifesto last night. It was delicious.

CRENSHAW. You're thinking of Antipasto.

CHEATO. No. Auntie Pasto married Uncle Linguini.

CRENSHAW. Sounds like a tasty marriage. Were they happy?

CHEATO. Right up until the accident.

CRENSHAW. What accident?

CHEATO. Uncle Linguini was standing so close to the oven, he burned his manicotti.

CRENSHAW. I can imagine how painful that must be.

CHEATO. No, you can't.

CRENSHAW. You're right. I can't... Well, at least he should be thankful he didn't scorch his meatballs. I can imagine how painful that would be.

CHEATO. No, you can't.

CRENSHAW. You're right. I can't.

HOBO. *(Honking his bicycle horn.)* Honk.

CRENSHAW. I guess he can't either.

CHEATO. Say, if you only getta nine votes, how come you getta be President?

CRENSHAW. I won in the Electoral College.

CHEATO. You can't fool me. You never went to college.

CRENSHAW. Of course, I did. I matriculated for years.

CHEATO. You what?

CRENSHAW. I matriculated.

CHEATO. Well, I wouldn'ta brag abouta that if I was you.

HOBO. *(Honking his bicycle horn.)* Honk. Honk.

CHEATO. He says, he wouldn't either.

CRENSHAW. I said matriculated. That means I went to college.

CHEATO. Matriculated. Hey, that's a real three-dollar word.

CRENSHAW. Yeah. But I bought it at a yard sale for a quarter.

CHEATO. That'sa funny. He bought his brain at a yard sale. They said it was fifty percent off.

HOBO. *(Honking his bicycle horn.)* Honk.

CRENSHAW. Talk about truth in advertising...

CHEATO. So, what college you go to?

CRENSHAW. Harvard.

CHEATO. Harvard University? That'sa good school.

CRENSHAW. No. Harvard Nagila. You might have heard of it. It's a small college, but our school song is very popular.

(He starts to hop around, singing the Jewish folk song "Hava Nagila")

CRENSHAW. *(Singing)*

HARVARD NAGILA
HARVARD NAGILA
HARVARD NAGILA
SO PROUD IS MY MOM!

CHEATO. Hokay. Hokay. So, you a big college man. If you so smart, how you gonna balance the budget?

CRENSHAW. Balance the budget? That's easy.

(Crenshaw picks up a thick binder balances it on one finger and spins it like a plate.)

CHEATO. Where you learn to balance a budget like that?

CRENSHAW. I was an accountant for the circus. I got used to juggling the books.

CHEATO. Lemme try.

(Cheato takes the thick binder and balances it on his head.)

CHEATO. (CONT'D) Hey. Lookit me! I'm under-budget! Now you try!

(Hobo puts the binder on his head. After some humorous pantomime. It falls off. He looks at it on the floor, then jumps on it.)

CHEATO. *(CONT'D)* Uh-oh. Looks like he's over-budget.

CRENSHAW. I thought he had a Deficit Attention Disorder.

CHEATO. Well, we gotta get back to Congress. They want us to vote on somethin' or other before we all heada home for vacation.

CRENSHAW. When does Congress break for vacation?

CHEATO. June.

CRENSHAW. But this is January.

CHEATO. *(Shrugs)* Hey, we gotta pack.

CRENSHAW. And they say you guys on Capitol Hill aren't productive...

CHEATO. They don't pay us to be productive. They pay us to spend lotsa money we don't have.

CRENSHAW. Sounds like my ex-wife. So, what kind of legislation are you voting on?

CHEATO. Crime-a bill.

(Hobo is pilfering small items from various points around the room. He shoves them into the pockets of his long trenchcoat.)

CRENSHAW. Looks like your friend is getting a head start.

CHEATO. He's just doin' a little research. I have a staff do mine for me. Mind if I usea you phone?

CRENSHAW. It's on the desk. Help yourself.

(They both dash over and start shoving everything from the desk into their pockets.)

CRENSHAW. *(CONT'D)* I said help yourself to the phone. Not everything that isn't tied down.

CHEATO. You know what they say, "God helpsa those who help themselves."

CRENSHAW. Well, God help you if the Secret Service catches you with all that.

CHEATO. Why? Can't they keep a secret?

CRENSHAW. I certainly hope so. You'll never believe what I did in the Lincoln Bedroom.

CHEATO. Which one is the hot line?

CRENSHAW. Line three.

(He picks up the receiver and drops it quickly.)

CHEATO. Yow! Hot line.

CRENSHAW. Tell me about it.

(Hobo pulls an oven mitt out of his trenchcoat and hands it to Cheato.)

CHEATO. *(Into phone.)* Yeah. Hello. I'ma thinkin' about takin' a sea cruise, but I'ma little worried about the food they serve on the ship. Lemme speak to the cruise chef. The Cruise chef... Kruschev... Kruschev... What he's dead? Does Yoko know? Yoko. It's what's in the middle of an Ital... oh. You heard that one... Well, no sense in Stalin. I gotta Putin an appearance at the Senate. Gorbachov to you, too. *(Hangs up.)* Geesh. You think after bein' in Poland for so many years, those guys woulda have a better sensa humor.

CRENSHAW. I hope you don't think this is rude, but didn't you say you have something important to pass?

CHEATO. Thanks for reminding me. Where's your little Senator's room?

CRENSHAW. Out that door. First tree on the left.

CHEATO. Arrivaderci.

CRENSHAW. "A river's dirty" to you too.

HOBO. *(Honking his bicycle horn.)* Honk.

CRENSHAW. I couldn't have said it better myself. Uh, I'd shake your hand, but I'm rather attached to my fingers.

(They dash out, Stage Left. Crenshaw walks over to the window UpStage Center and appears to be watching them out on the White House lawn.)

CRENSHAW. *(CONT'D)* I sure hope the Secret Service keeps sharpshooters on the grounds.

(Jorden and Jessica enter.)

JORDEN. Mr. President?

CRENSHAW. Where? Oh...that's me!

JESSICA. Are you all right, sir? You seem rather pensive.

CRENSHAW. Do I? It must be because I was born in Pensivvannia. What are you doing here? Can't you see I'm busy… uh, presidenting?

JESSICA. Presiding, sir.

CRENSHAW. Well, if I can find the time, I'll do that, too.

JORDEN. We came to tell you that your cabinet has arrived.

CRENSHAW. I don't have time for my cabinet now. I'm already seeing my desk on the side, and I'm supposed to sneak out and wrestle my armchair in the sitting room. Then I have a conference with my table, and an appointment with my special console. Not to mention my credenza...

JESSICA. Your credenza?

CRENSHAW. Shhhh! I told you not to mention it. (whispers) You know how jealous the vanity can get!

JESSICA. I don't think you understand, sir. Your cabinet is your panel of trusted advisors. Most were carried over from the previous administration.

CRENSHAW. So, who locked these people in the cabinet?

JESSICA. They're not in the cabinet. They are the cabinet. You know, the Secretary of State. The Secretary of Defense. The Secretary of Treasury. You know.

CRENSHAW. Oh. That cabinet! Why didn't you say so? You should be ashamed of your shelf. Remember, it's your job to furnish me with information. By the way, have I mentioned what a nice chest you have?

JESSICA. Mr. President! I will not allow myself to be the victim of your juvenile double entendres!

CRENSHAW. Then send in someone who will. Call the first lady.

JORDEN. You are not married, Mr. President.

CRENSHAW. Then send in the first lady you can find. And send in the second and third while you're at it. I have the Clinton legacy to live up to. Now, if you'll excuse me for a moment, I just remembered an appointment with the Nixon Bathroom.

(Crenshaw dashes out Stage Left. Jessica plops down on the sofa.)

JESSICA. I don't think I can take four years of this, Jorden... It gets harder and harder with each administration.

JORDEN. I know what you mean. When I first came to Washington, I dreamed of working with the best and brightest. Men and women who cared about solving our nation's problems.

JESSICA. ...instead of this torpid class of bloated plutocrats!

JORDEN. Could you translate that? I forgot to bring my Thesaurus.

JESSICA. Sorry. It's my official spokesman side coming out... Official spokesman side...I hate myself for even admitting I have a side like that...

JORDEN. You're way too hard on yourself, Jessica. You are the best there is. Nobody in Washington can hoodwink the media like you. Nobody can match you metaphor for metaphor. Or is it simile for simile?

JESSICA. You are not making me feel any better.

JORDEN. Sound bite for sound bite?

JESSICA. The funny thing is...I always dreamed I would write the Great American novel. Instead, I spout the Great American Lie. Deluding a hopeful nation into believing the system still works. And that politicians still try to do what's right, instead of what's politically expedient.

JORDEN. I still believe that.

JESSICA. Like I said, you're a boy scout. Last of a dying breed.

JORDEN. Is that such a bad thing?

JESSICA. Maybe not. But for the rest of the country has devolved into a Twitter democracy. Government for The Short Attention Span. And we have no one to blame but ourselves.

JORDEN. I wonder what our founding fathers would have thought of all this…?

As the lights dim and the music begins to swell. Jorden looks at the portrait of George Washington and begins to sing.

"WHAT WOULD GEORGE WASHINGTON THINK?"

JORDEN. *(Singing)*

WHAT WOULD GEORGE WASHINGTON THINK?
TO SEE US TODAY ON THE BRINK?
WHEN THOSE WE ELECTED
SEEM SPECIFICALLY SELECTED
BASED ON HOW WELL THEY LIE, CHEAT AND DRINK.

JESSICA. *(Singing)*

NOW WHAT WOULD HONEST ABE SAY?
OF A GOVERNMENT GONE SO FAR ASTRAY?
THERE'S A CLASS OF NOBILITY
WE RE-ELECT 'TIL SENILITY
WITH THE POWER TO RAISE THEIR OWN PAY.

JORDEN & JESSICA *(Singing)*

OH, THOSE DREAMS AND BELIEFS THAT THEY FOUGHT FOR
IN THOSE DAYS OF REBELLION AND STRIFE
THEIR LOFTY IDEALS
DETERMINATION OF STEEL
FORGED THE AMERICAN WAY OF LIFE.
(THE AMERICAN WAY OF LIFE)

JESSICA. *(Singing)*

COULD JEFFERSON DO ANYTHING BUT LAUGH?
AT EACH CURRENT MISSTATEMENT AND GAFFE
WOULD HE SPIN IN HIS GRAVE
AT THE VISION HE GAVE
NOW FILLED WITH CORRUPTION AND GRAFT?

JORDEN and JESSICA. *(Singing)*

OH, THOSE DREAMS AND BELIEFS THAT THEY FOUGHT FOR
IN DAYS OF REBELLION AND STRIFE
OUR FAITH IN THE SPINELESS
BUREAUCRACY MINDLESS
TO BANKRUPT THE AMERICAN WAY OF LIFE
(THE AMERICAN WAY OF LIFE)

JORDEN & JESSICA. *(Singing)*

IS THERE ANYTHING BRAVE MEN COULD SAY
AFTER TWO HUNDRED YEARS OF DECAY?
YET WITH EACH ADMINISTRATION
WE HOPE FOR SALVATION
AND FOR SOMEONE TO SHOW US THE WAY.
FOR SOMEONE TO SHOW US THE WAY...

CRENSHAW. *(Entering.)* Did someone call me?

JESSICA. Um...No, sir. Jorden and I were merely reflecting on our founding fathers.

CRENSHAW. I didn't know you were born in a foundry. Then again, I try not to metal in other people's affairs. Although you should never discount the benefits of an occasional affair. Care for a cigar?

JORDEN. We were talking about the founding fathers of the country, sir. George Washington, Thomas Jefferson...

CRENSHAW. The guy on the one-dollar bill, and the guy on the nickel. Which reminds me. What do I have to do to get my face on some money?

JORDEN. You have to be dead first.

CRENSHAW. Then I'll settle for getting my hands on some. Why are you wasting your time with a bunch of old dead guys anyway?

JESSICA. They say those who don't know history are doomed to repeat it.

CRENSHAW. They say the same thing about those who eat old chili. As for you, Miss Woodard. I'm putty in your hands.

(He falls into her arms. She pushes him away.)

JESSICA. Mr. President, please! You have a photo op in the Rose Garden in five minutes. The media wants pictures of the new president.

CRENSHAW. Pictures? You mean like for a security badge? Can I get one of those little ID badges? I promise to put my real name on it this time.

JESSICA. Mister President. Please stay focused.

CRENSHAW. Isn't that the photographer's job? Don't tell me I have to do his work, too?

JESSICA. All you have to do is stand in the Rose Garden and wave to the cameras. No contact. No speeches. Just let them take your picture.

CRENSHAW. Okay, but walk behind me. *(Wiggles his butt.)* That way you can keep an eye on my best side!

(Crenshaw exits Stage Left. Before she follows him off, Jessica throws an exasperated look to Jorden, who can only shrug. She turns, horrified.)

JESSICA. *(Calling offstage.)* Mister President! You can't do that in the rose bushes!!! The cameras are rolling!

(She dashes off, Stage Left. Alone in the Oval Office, Jorden shakes his head. He walks over to the desk and picks up a ceremonial gavel given to the White House by a former Supreme Court justice. He rubs the gavel thoughtfully, walks over to the picture of Thomas Jefferson and sings, almost to himself.)

JORDEN. *(Despondently)*

WHAT WOULD OUR FOREFATHERS THINK...?

(His quiet reverie is disturbed by a loud KNOCK on the door. Caught off-guard, he shoves the gavel in his pants pocket, and crosses Stage Right to open the door. MAE WAIST enters. She is 40, blonde and buxom. and looks eerily similar to sexpot comedienne Mae West, filled with double entendres and aggressive sensuality.)

MAE WAIST. Why, hello there, Fletcher. Is that a gavel in your pocket, or are you happy to see me?

JORDEN. Mae... uh, I mean, Miss Waist... How did you get past the military guard?

MAE WAIST. I paraded my formation in front of them, and those boys were kind enough to stand at attention. *(Pushing her way into the room.)* I love men in uniform. I even love men when they're out of their uniforms. In fact, that's when I love them better. Oooh.

JORDEN. Miss Waist, President Sparx has only been in power one day. I don't think he has time for lobbyists!

MAE WAIST. If I make time for him, he can make time for me. I'm sure he'll find making time with me a worthwhile investment. Oooh. He tries to maneuver her toward the door.

JORDEN. I must insist. The president has no time for special interests today.

MAE WAIST. Oooh. You're so cute when you try to be assertive. *(Playing with his lapels.)* That's what you're trying to be, isn't it? A big, strong man like you trying to have his way with little old me?

JORDEN. No... Not really... I mean, yes! My job is to control the President's calendar and see that everything runs smoothly.

MAE WAIST. Then you better try harder because it feels like you're losing your grip. I can help you practice that grip. All you have to do is pencil me in.

(She throws her arms around the hapless Jorden and kisses him passionately, pinning him against the wall. Jessica and Crenshaw enter, Stage Left.)

JESSICA. Jorden Fletcher!

CRENSHAW. Looks like I wasn't the only one being led down the garden path.

JORDEN. I... I'm sorry, Mister President. I was um…checking Miss Waist's... uh, credentials.

CRENSHAW. She certainly has a nice set of them.

MAE WAIST. Why thank you, Mister President.

CRENSHAW. And he sure seemed to be checking them very thoroughly. Wouldn't you say, Miss Woodard?

JESSICA. *(With venom.)* Very thoroughly, sir.

JORDEN. I'm sorry, Miss Waist. As I uh, said, the President's schedule is far too busy. You will have to leave immediately!

CRENSHAW. What's the rush? *(To Mae Waist.)* Hi. I'm President of the United States. Most powerful man in America. I control the lives of three hundred and seventy million people. How's that for an opening line?

MAE WAIST. You deliver it well.

CRENSHAW. Oh, you're just trying to butter me up.

MAE WAIST. Perceptive, too.

JESSICA. Mister President. It would not be to your advantage if the media found you meeting with special interests after only a few hours in office...

CRENSHAW. Handling the media is your job, Miss Woodard. Taking advantage is mine. Why don't you and Mr. Floosie...

JORDEN. Fletcher.

CRENSHAW. Why don't you two go off and schedule something for me. I'll handle Miss Waist.

MAE WAIST. Think you can handle me, Mr. President?

CRENSHAW. I'm willing to give it the old college try. I'm somewhat of a freshman.

MAE WAIST. They're all fresh the first time you unwrap them.

JESSICA. Mister President. I really must insist!

MAE WAIST. You still here, Miss Woodard?

(Realizing they've lost the battle, Jorden reaches for Jessica's elbow.)

JESSICA. Don't you touch me. Mr. Floosie!

JORDEN. Fletcher!

JESSICA. Whatever…

(She storms off R, slamming the door behind her. Jorden follows sheepishly.)

CRENSHAW. That's funny. I was about to say the exact opposite to you.

MAE WAIST. Mister President, you're going to make me blush.

(Throughout the following, Crenshaw and Mae Waist chase each other around the set in a humorous 'cat-and-mouse' romantic pursuit. Mae Waist is the aggressor, and Crenshaw her all-too-willing victim.)

CRENSHAW. I'll bet my mustache you haven't blushed in years.

MAE WAIST. Only when it gets me what I want.

CRENSHAW. Is that so? And what is it you want?

MAE WAIST. I'm a lobbyist. I get paid to…influence you.

(She backs him to the sofa. Pushes him down, then sits beside him.)

CRENSHAW. Is that what they call it these days? It's so hard to keep up with the vernacular. *(Puts his head on her lap like a puppy.)* So, who do you lobby for? Wall Street?

MAE WAIST. They couldn't afford me.

CRENSHAW. The NRA?

MAE WAIST. A bunch of big shots. I like men of larger caliber.

CRENSHAW. Small Business Administration?

MAE WAIST. I don't handle anything with the word 'small' in it.

CRENSHAW. Teacher's Union?

MAE WAIST. Not enough class.

CRENSHAW. Dock workers?

MAE WAIST. I do them on my own time.

(She grabs him in a bosomy embrace. He glances at her ample chest.)

CRENSHAW. Um...Milk Producers of America?

MAE WAIST. How did you know?

CRENSHAW. Lucky guess.... So, what exactly can I do to you...uh, I mean, for you, Miss Waist? It is Miss Waist, isn't it? There isn't a Mister Waist running around, is there?

MAE WAIST. There was a Mister Waist, but he died.

CRENSHAW. How did he die?

MAE WAIST. Happy.

CRENSHAW. *(Gulps)* Did I mention I have close to unlimited power?

MAE WAIST. Then a big, strong President like you won't have any problem pushing one little itty bitty subsidy bill through Congress for me, would he?

CRENSHAW. Uh, what itty bitty subsidy?

MAE WAIST. Just some teensy-weensy old price supports.

CRENSHAW. Explain price supports to me. Assume I don't know anything.

MAE WAIST. I assumed that from the first moment I saw you.

CRENSHAW. Well then… Hey!

MAE WAIST. You know how the government pays farmers not to grow wheat to keep crop prices from crashing? My people want to be paid not to milk cows, to keep their hands from chaffing.

CRENSHAW. A little teat for tat, huh?

MAE WAIST. Can I count on your support?

CRENSHAW. *(Looking at her chest.)* I don't know. There's a lot there to support. Besides, won't that mean little kids will have to pay more for their milk?

MAE WAIST. Sure. But all those extra pennies could wind up in the pocket of your re-election campaign. Or maybe even your own pocket. Besides, aren't some things worth a little extra attention?

(She kisses him passionately. His foot raises off the floor. When she lets him go, he has a dazed and dopey smile on his face, as if his libido just short-circuited.)

CRENSHAW. *(Dreamily)* Uh, where do I sign?

MAE WAIST. You don't have to sign anything. I'll go tell those boys in Congress that you're going to support my legislation. And if they fight it, they'll have to answer to you.

CRENSHAW. *(Still entranced.)* Yeah. They'll have to answer to me...

(She stands up suddenly, spilling him onto the floor.)

MAE WAIST. Thank you, Mister President. It was a business doing pleasure with you.

CRENSHAW. Hey! When do I get my big pay-off?!

MAE WAIST. If you're lucky, I'll show up in the next act.

(She exits, Stage Right. Crenshaw collapses happily onto the sofa.)

CRENSHAW. I think I'm in love! Not only that, I've just earned a second revenue stream. Isn't Washington wonderful!

(Jorden enters, concerned.)

JORDEN. Mister President?

CRENSHAW. Come on in, Fletcher. Tell me, do I look particularly irresistible today?

JORDEN. Sir?

CRENSHAW. Miss Waist seems to think so.

JORDEN. Please excuse my directness, sir. But she is a paid lobbyist, after all.

CRENSHAW. Are you saying she only wants to seduce me, so I'll help some special interest group?

JORDEN. It is a possibility, sir.

CRENSHAW. I can live with that. You don't like her very much, do you, Fletcher?

JORDEN. It's not that I don't like her. I've seen how she operates. And I think you'll find she has her own agenda.

CRENSHAW. Well, from everything I saw, her 'genda' is decidedly female.

"MORE THAN THE SUM OF HER PARTS"

CRENSHAW. *(Singing)*

SHE'S MORE THAN THE SUM OF HER PARTS
I HARDLY KNOW WHERE TO START
HER LIPS ARE ENTRANCING
HER HIPS SET ME DANCING
SHE'S MORE THAN THE SUM OF HER PARTS

SHE'S MORE THAN THE SUM OF HER PARTS
HER FIGURE IS WAY OFF THE CHARTS
A WOMAN LIKE THAT
COULD LAY A GUY FLAT
SHE'S MORE THAN THE SUM OF HER PARTS

SHE'S A HOTTIE WITH A BODY
THAT'S NOT EASILY IGNORED
HER DEMEANOR IS OBSCENER
ONCE YOU'VE SEEN HER, OH MY LORD!
SHE'S A LADY SLIGHTLY SHADY
BUT THE WAY SHE MAKES ME FEEL
IS ALL SQUIGGLY, SLIGHTLY GIGGLY
WHEN SHE'S WRIGGLY, IT'S UNREAL

SHE'S MORE THAN THE SUM OF HER PARTS
BUILT TO MANHANDLE MEN'S HEARTS
LET ME BE SPECIFIC
HER BREASTS ARE TERRIFIC!
SHE'S MORE THAN THE SUM OF HER PARTS

MORE

CRENSHAW. *(Singing)*

THOUGH I ADMIT I'M A BIG FAN OF HER PARTS
SHE'S MORE THAN THE SUM OF HER PARTS

JORDEN. I urge caution, Mr. President.

CRENSHAW. I'll be as cautious as a blonde in a horror movie. And speaking of dismemberment, did you patch things up with Miss Woodheart, yet?

JORDEN. Miss Woodard?

CRENSHAW. You know…, that vixen of vocabulary. That sultry siren of speechmaking. She seemed pretty upset when you left. Looked like jealousy to me.

JORDEN. Her reaction did seem a bit...extreme.

CRENSHAW. Take my word for it. When she saw Mae Waist making eyes at me, it was more than Jessica's innocent heart could bear. It's hard being a stud muffin, Fletcher. Be grateful you don't have to suffer with these looks.

JORDEN. I was glad of that from the first moment I saw your face, sir.

CRENSHAW. I imagine so, I... *(Suddenly.)* Say, that sounded pretty close to sarcasm. You're not concealing a sense of humor in there, are you, Fletcher?

JORDEN. No, sir. I wouldn't dream of disrespecting your office.

CRENSHAW. Good. My office is very sensitive. The rug already feels walked all over and the wallpaper is pretty thin-skinned. See that it doesn't happen again.

JORDEN. Yes, Mr. President.

CRENSHAW. Now, who's my first appointment?

JORDEN. That would be Mr. Subsidy. Secretary of Health and Human Services.

CRENSHAW. Health and Human Services? Hmmm. Do we have a Secretary for Wealth and Inhuman Services?

JORDEN. That would be the Internal Revenue Service.

CRENSHAW. There's that sense of humor again, Fletcher. One more joke like that and I'll have to transfer you to the Department of Redundancy Department.

(Crenshaw straightens his clothes after his lusty encounter with Miss Waist.)

CRENSHAW. *(CONT'D)* Okay. Send in this Mr. Subsidy. But give me a moment to freshen up.

(Jorden exits, Stage Right. Crenshaw pulls a flask out of his coat pocket and takes a deep swallow.)

CRENSHAW. *(CONT'D)* Ahhhh. Refreshing!

(He dabs some of the liquor under his arms and behind his ears. The Stage Right door swings open, and in tumbles Cheato and Hobo.)

CRENSHAW. *(CONT'D)* Don't I know you?

CHEATO. I'm Vito Subsidy. Secretary of Health and Human Services.

CRENSHAW. I thought you were in the Senate?

CHEATO. I am. I wear two hats.

(He lifts off his cap to reveal a smaller one underneath. Hobo lifts off his top hat, revealing an even tinier hat.)

CHEATO. *(CONT'D)* He wears two hats, too.

CRENSHAW. So, you're in my cabinet, eh?

CHEATO. That'sa right. Health and Human Services. Anybody you need serviced?

CRENSHAW. Well, most of the people I know are broke, or in a fix. Who's he?

(Hobo dives on the floor by Cheato's feet. Cheato rests one foot on his back.)

CHEATO. He's the Under-secretary.

CRENSHAW. You guys will do anything for a punchline, won't you?

CHEATO. Just about. You should see our new Health Care plan.

CRENSHAW. Tell me about it. Although, I probably couldn't stop you if I wanted to.

CHEATO. We spenta lotsa time working on this new Health Plan... Ten, maybe twelve minutes.

HOBO. *(Honking his bicycle horn.)* Honk.

CHEATO. Okay, Maybe five. But it'sa like this. We pay for everybody in the country to get alla the health care they need, whenever they want it. Everybody except the Hippocataracts...

CRENSHAW. You mean the hypochondriacs.

CHEATO. No, them we cover. Under our plan, you wanna go see a doctor, you go see a doctor. You wanna go see a dentist, you go see a dentist. You wanna go see a psychiatrist, they make you a politician.

CRENSHAW. I resemble that remark.

CHEATO. You wanna go see a foot doctor, you step right up. You wanna go see a chiropractor, you get cracking. You wanna go to an eye doctor, you see him, too. You wanna see a heart doctor, you just drive your Cardiac right up to the door.

CRENSHAW. You don't miss a beat. What if I wanna see a proctologist?

CHEATO. Oh, you don't wanna see onea those, trust me. He usedta be a proctologist.

HOBO. *(Honking his bicycle horn.)* Honk.

CRENSHAW. He usedta be a proctologist? Why'd he quit?

HOBO. *(Honking his bicycle horn.)* Honk.

CHEATO. *(Holding up his index finger.)* He said he had it up to here. Putta that finger down, Hobo.

CRENSHAW. I get the picture...though I'd rather not. It sounds like a great Health Plan. How much does it cost?

CHEATO. It don't costa penny. You go to as many doctors asa you want. We cover everybody in the country for free.

CRENSHAW. Sounds great. How is the country going to pay for it?

CHEATO. Pay for it?

(He turns to Hobo, as if he never considered this idea before. Hobo looks equally confused.)

HOBO. *(Honking his bicycle horn.)* Honk…?

CHEATO. We, uh... we ain't worked out alla details, yet.

CRENSHAW. You two have a promising future in Washington.

CHEATO. Hey. We gotta go now. We're wanted on Capitol Hill.

CRENSHAW. I bet you guys are wanted in all fifty states.

CHEATO. Fifty states? You hear that, Hobo? Now we got fifty states. I thought Obama said fifty-seven. Well, we gotta fly.

CRENSHAW. *(Swatting the air.)* Looks like you got more than one. I hear bathing helps.

CHEATO. Naw. Tried it once. Didn't take.

CRENSHAW. Don't worry. I doubt you are the only dirty politician I'll see today.

(Jessica and Jorden enter Stage Right.)

JORDEN. Mr. President?

CRENSHAW & CHEATO. *(Together.)* Yes?

HOBO. *(Honking his bicycle horn.)* Honk?

CRENSHAW. Back off. This is my scam!

CHEATO. We wasa just leavin'.

CRENSHAW. *(Notices Hobo pilfering.)* So are most of my possessions. Excuse me. You forgot to steal the table.

CHEATO. He'll be back for that later.

(Cheato and Hobo exit, Stage Left.)

CRENSHAW. It's politicians like them that give the rest of us a bad name. But enough about them, let's talk about me. How can this presidential racket earn me some real moola?

JESSICA. Sir?

CRENSHAW. What's the inside angle? Who's got who's fingers in who's pocket?

JORDEN. May I remind you, sir, you already receive a sizable salary for being President. And when you add in speaking fees after you leave office, it is not inconceivable that you will retire a multi-millionaire.

CRENSHAW. A multi-millionaire, eh? I like the sound of that. 'Course I'd like the sound of it more if it could happen by Thursday.

JESSICA. Sir, I believe you should worry less about personal wealth and more about your public image.

CRENSHAW. Way ahead of you, Woodhead. I just had my nose hair styled.

JESSICA. That's an attractive image, sir. However, I was talking about an issue to define your administration.

CRENSHAW. I don't need another issue. I get Bikinis Monthly every week. Sometimes I even go to the library after lunch so I can hear the Readers Digest.

JESSICA. Not that kind of issue, Mr. President. A political issue. A problem of national importance which deeply concerns you. It is a good way to position yourself with the voters.

CRENSHAW. There are lots of ways I can position myself... I can position myself like this...

(He throws himself across his desktop and winks flirtatiously.)

CRENSHAW. *(CONT'D)* ... Or like this...

(He leaps up and executes an equally ridiculous pose on the sofa.)

CRENSHAW. *(CONT'D)* ...Or even like this!

(He jumps up and bends over as if to 'moon' the audience. Luckily, Jorden stops him before he can drop his pants.)

JORDEN. I think what Ms. Woodard means...is that we need an issue to define your administration in the eyes of the public. Like welfare reform... the budget... or education.

CRENSHAW. Hey! That's good. Can you see me as The Education President?

JORDEN. It would be a stretch, sir.

CRENSHAW. Maybe I can concentrate on the decline in family values. Then I'd be the 'Vice' President. Or crime. Can you see me as The Crime President?

JORDEN. Far easier to imagine, sir.

JESSICA. There are so many important issues facing our country. Terrorism... drugs... jobs... the environment...

CRENSHAW. The environment? You mean like hugging trees and animals?

JESSICA. It's a bit more involved than that, sir.

CRENSHAW. The Environmental President. I like that. Everybody knows I love animals. I once rescued an elephant in my pajamas. How it got in my pajamas, I'll never know. *(To audience.)* Sometimes we even recycle the jokes...

JESSICA. The environment is a wise choice, Mr. President. The latest polls show climate change is a hot issue. By taking a firm stand, you can gain a lot of political mileage. We could even build your reelection campaign around it.

CRENSHAW. I'm here one day, and we're already planning my reelection?

JORDEN. *(Wryly)* Welcome to Washington, sir.

CRENSHAW. Okay. Global warming. Am I for it or against it?

JESSICA. I suggest being against it, sir.

CRENSHAW. Okay, I'm against it. I'm against dirty air, dirty rivers and dirty dirt. And oil spills and landfills and oceans swimming in plastic. Wait, I think I hear a song in there...

(The music swells as Crenshaw breaks into a Calypso song with his typical manic style and schizophrenic energy.)

"THE CLIMES THEY ARE A'CHANGIN'"

CRENSHAW. *(Singing.)*

IN THE OCEAN
I'VE A NOTION
THAT IT'S GETTING' HOTTER
CALIFORNIA
LET ME WARN YA
WE'RE RUNNIN' OUTTA WATER

MISSISSIPPI
IS MORE DRIPPY
RIVERS WILL BE RISIN'
DAT POLLUTION
AIN'T NO SOLUTION
DAT I AM SURMISIN'

(Jorden & Jessica join in happy that they have given the President a cause.)

JESSICA & JORDEN. *(Singing.)*

FEEL DA HEAT
IN DA STREET
TEMP'RATURES ARE SOARIN'
DA NORTH POLE
NO LONGER SO COL'
POLAR BEAR IS ROARIN'

CRENSHAW. *(Singing.)*

GREENHOUSE SMOKIN' HAS US CHOKIN'
I'M NOT JOKIN'.
THE PLANET'S BROKEN!

ALL ABOUT
THE PEOPLE DOUBT
EXPERTS LECTURE.
PURE CONJECTURE
THEY EXPECT YOUR
TIME'S RUN OUT
LISTEN HOW THEY RANT AND SHOUT

ALL. *(Singing.)*
OH, THE CLIMES THEY ARE A'CHANGIN'

CRENSHAW. *(Singing.)*

FEAR DA WARMIN'
INCREASED STORMIN'
THEY SAY THE END IS NEAR!
WHO WILL PROSPER
FROM DE PHOSPHOR
IN OUR ATMOSPHERE?

ALL. *(Singing.)*

GLOBAL WARMIN'
IS TRANSFORMIN'
OUR ENVIRONMENT-YEAH
NOTHIN' TO IT?
BUT DID WE DO IT?
DAT'S DE ARGUMENT-YEAH

CRENSHAW. *(Singing.)*

GREENHOUSE SMOKIN' HAS US CHOKIN'
I'M NOT JOKIN'.
THE PLANET'S BROKEN!

CRENSHAW. *(Singing.)*

ARCTIC HEATIN'
ICE RETREATIN'
PENGUINS CHASE A
MELTIN' GLACIER
JUST IN CASE YA
ATTENTION'S FLEETIN'
THIS PRESIDENT
WILL HOLD A MEETIN'

ALL. *(Singing.)*

'CAUSE THE CLIMES THEY ARE A'CHANGIN'

(The three collapse on the sofa. Jessica and Jorden are thrilled. Maybe there's something to this new President after all. Suddenly, Crenshaw jumps up.)

CRENSHAW. Now that we got that's settled, I want you to schedule an appointment with the head of the EPA. I want to get off to a fast start, or I'm not the Environmental President.

JESSICA. Yes, sir!

(She starts to leave but turns just as she reaches the door.)

JESSICA. *(CONT'D)* Mr. President, I can't tell you how excited I am to see you dedicating your administration to such an important issue!

CRENSHAW. That's what they pay me for, Miss Woodard.

(She exits happily. Then...)

CRENSHAW. *(CONT'D)* But they don't pay me enough, Fletcher. I want you to figure out a way for me to skim some serious moulah off this environmental scam.

JORDEN. But you said…?

CRENSHAW. Remember the words of John F. Kennedy, "Ask not what you can do for your country. Ask what your country can do for you."

JORDEN. I believe it was the other way around, sir,

CRENSHAW. Needed an update in the post-Trump years. *(Singing.)*

I'LL PREACH THE TOPIC LIKE I'M A PROPHET
WHILE SOME MAY SCOFF
I'LL GET RICH OFF IT
MAKE A PROFIT
SOME SHADY DEALS ARRANGIN'!
NOW THAT THE CLIMES THEY ARE A'CHANGIN'

CRENSHAW. *(CONT'D)* You know, I'm really starting to like this presidenting gig, Fletcher. So, what other appointments do I have this act?

JORDEN. The Joint Chiefs of Staff are scheduled to be here any minute.

CRENSHAW. The Joint Chiefs? What are they? Executives with big knuckles?

JORDEN. The Joint Chiefs are the senior officers in charge of each branch of the military. In your role as Commander...

CRENSHAW. I thought I was the President?

JORDEN. The President also serves as Commander-In-Chief of the Armed Forces.

CRENSHAW. Me, in charge of the entire US military? *(To audience.)* I bet you'll all sleep better knowing that... *(To Jorden.)* Well, send them in. We don't want to keep the Joint Chiefs out in the cold. They could develop a Staff infection. And remember what I said, there's money in being green!

JORDEN. Whatever you say, Mister President...

(He exits, shaking his head. Crenshaw stuffs a few more valuables in his pockets. He stops, looks over his shoulder, up at the portrait of Lincoln.)

CRENSHAW. A penny for your thoughts, Abe.

(A KNOCK)

CRENSHAW. *(CONT'D)* Come in!

(The Joint Chiefs enter. BARRY, BO & CURBEY are the Three Stupids. If we didn't know better, we might swear they were The Three Stooges - Larry. Moe and Curly. They try to cram through the doorway all at once. Of course, they can't fit through the opening like that.)

BO. Spread out!

(He BOPS each on the head in classic Stooges form. NOTE: Offstage sound effects could enhance these segments with various clunks, whomps and bongs. After a few painful bops and eye pokes, they notice Crenshaw standing by the desk. All three step forward and salute comically, Bo in the middle.)

BO. *(CONT'D)* Your highness!

BARRY. Your majesty!

CURBEY. You're appendix! Yuck yuck yuck.

CRENSHAW. Gentlemen. And I use that term loosely...

(They all share salutes. However, since they are standing so close to each other, Barry and Curbey's rapid salutes smash their elbows into Bo's chin. He responds by simultaneously hitting each in the stomach. As they both bend forward, he bops each on the head.)

BO. Straighten up! Can't you see we're with the President of the United States?

CURBEY. Coiytainly. *(Salutes again.)* General Nuisance of the Army.

BARRY. General Disturbance. Marines.

BO. And I'm Admiral Dishwasher.

CRENSHAW. Sounds like a Private Joke to me. Where's the Air Force guy?

CURBEY. He just took off. Yuck, yuck, yuck.

BO. Show some respect. We're just Joint Chiefs. He's the Commander in Chief.

CURBEY. Oh, the Chief Chief, eh?

(He starts doing a war dance, followed by Barry and Bo.)

CRENSHAW. *(To audience)* I can't tell you how politically incorrect that was.

BO. Sir. The two million men and women of the Armed Forces stand ready to do your bidding!

BARRY. His bedding? Why does it take two million soldiers to do his bedding?

CURBEY. He must be a real big sheet.

(Bo whacks them with a few more classic Stooges moves.)

BO. His bidding, you imbeciles. Not his bedding!

CURBEY. Why didn't you say so?

BARRY. Anyone you want us to invade, Mister President?

CRENSHAW. How about New Jersey?

CURBEY. No, thanks. This old uniform will be fine. Yuck, yuck, yuck.

CRENSHAW. How do the boys at the Pentagon feel about NATO?

BARRY. I like mine with lots of cheese and Jalepeno.

BO. That's nachos, you idiot!

(Bonk!)

CRENSHAW. Any new threats from the third world?

CURBEY. I thought we were the third world... Mercury, Venus, Earth...

BO. Are we under attack from Mars, Mister President?

CRENSHAW. No. But when the spaceships come, you'll be the first ones I'll call.

CURBEY. Goody! Nobody can stand up to the good old US Army!

(The following dialogue is spoken in a rapid Three Stooges chant.)

BARRY. WAR WITH IRAQ?

CURBEY. WE'LL COUNTERATTACK!

BO. A THREAT FROM KOREA?

CURBEY. WE'LL SHOW THEM WHO WE-ARE!

BARRY. AN INVASION FROM CHINA?

CURBEY. WE'LL GIVE 'EM A SHINER!

BO. A BATTLE WITH BRITAIN?

CURBEY. WE'LL BE FIGHTIN' AND SPITTIN'!

BARRY. THE COMMUNIST BLOC?

CURBEY. WE'LL CLEAN THEIR CLOCK!

BO. A WAR WITH ALBANIA?

CURBEY. WE'LL FIGHT WITH A MANIA!

BARRY. A NEW GERMAN REICH?

CURBEY. ONE MASSIVE AIR STRIKE!

BO. TERRORISTS FROM LIBYA?

CURBEY. WE'LL FRACTURE THEIR TIBIA!

BARRY. A BATTLE WITH BELGIUM?

CURBEY. WE'LL SQUISH 'EM AND SQUELCH 'EM!

BO. A NEW THREAT FROM MOSCOW?

CURBEY. WE'LL SHOW 'EM WHO'S BOSS NOW!

BARRY. WARLORDS IN SOMALIA?

CURBEY. THEY'LL GET SMALLER AND SMALLIA!

BO. A FIGHT WITH JAPAN?

CURBEY. WE'LL KICK IN THEIR CAN!

BO. REVOLT IN THE CONGO?

CURBEY. WE'LL BEAT 'EM LIKE BONGOS!

BARRY. A SKIRMISH WITH FRANCE?

CURBEY. THEY WON'T STAND A CHANCE!

BO. ATTACK FROM AUSTRALIA?

CURBEY. IT'S US WHO'LL PREVAIL, YEAH!

BARRY. SOME TROUBLE WITH GREECE?

CURBEY. WE'LL TEAR 'EM TO PIECE... UH, EZ.

BO. A FORCE FROM TIBET?

CURBEY. YOU AIN'T SCARED ME YET!

BARRY. THE HUNS OF MONGOLIA?

CURBEY. WE'LL BE OUTA CONTROL-IA.

BO. THE MEXICAN ARMY?

CURBEY. NO WAY THEY CAN HARM ME.

BARRY. A CLASH WITH QUEBEC?

CURBEY. WE'LL KEEP 'EM IN CHECK.

BO. A DUEL WITH ZIMBABWE?

CURBEY. THEY WON'T GET IN OUR WAY!

BARRY. A SKIRMISH WITH SPAIN?

CURBEY. WE'LL GIVE 'EM SOME PAIN!

BO. HOSTILITIES WITH HOLLAND?

CURBEY. *(Breaks the rhythm.)* We'll…uh, surrender.

BO. Surrender? Why?

CURBEY. I don't want to fight anyone with wooden shoes. You know how much it hurts if they kick you?

BO. Yeah. It'd feel like this!

(Bo kicks Curbey, who dances around holding his shin.)

CURBEY. Yeoww! Oww! Oww!

BARRY. Don't hit him!

BO. Why not?

BARRY. 'Cause that'd be Corporal Punishment!

BO. Corporal Punishment...Very funny. But not as funny as this!

(He traps Barry in a head lock under his right arm. He grabs Curbey's head in a similar manner under his other arm.)

BARRY. Oww! Letgo!

CURBEY. Bo, Owww!

BO. Why I oughtta…

CRENSHAW. Excuse me... Excuse me...

BO. Sorry, Mister President. *(To others.)* Spread out!

CRENSHAW. Uh...General Nuisance, what's that in your pocket?

(Curbey pulls a grenade out of his pocket to show the others.)

CURBEY. An avocado. I picked it up at the Pentagon salad bar. I'm gonna make guacamole!

BO. The Pentagon doesn't have a salad bar, you idiot! And that avocado is going to make guacamole out of us!

BARRY. It's a grenade!

CURBEY. *(Juggling it.)* A grenade? Nyaaa-aaaa-aaa!

CRENSHAW. Don't worry. Grenades can't explode unless you pull the pin.

BARRY. What pin?

CURBEY. *(Pulling the pin.)* *I* think he means this one.

BO. Nyaaaa-aaaa-aaa!

(Realizing his mistake, Curbey tosses the grenade to Bo, who tosses it to Barry, who tosses it back to Curbey. They react with distinctive Three Stooges sounds and expressions of fear.)

CRENSHAW. Right this way, gentlemen.

(Crenshaw opens the door, Stage Left, and the trio run out in a panic, still tossing the grenade back and forth. After they exit, a loud BOOM echoes from offstage.)

CRENSHAW. *(CONT'D)* Whoever said 'Old soldiers just fade away' never had to clean up what's left of those guys.

(Jorden and Jessica rush in, Stage Right.)

JORDEN. Mister President, Are you all right?!

CRENSHAW. I think so. Although I have this strange rash from my boxer shorts...

JESSICA. What was that explosion?!

CRENSHAW. Just a little blow-up at the Pentagon. I'd say the Joint Chiefs are pretty disjointed at the moment.

JESSICA. Mr. President. Do you realize what this means?!

CRENSHAW. Yes. (solemnly) We now have three less stooges in Washington.

(The soft refrain of the THREE STOOGES THEME SONG.*)*

CRENSHAW. (CONT'D) I suppose I should go out there and say something meaningful. Something touching and respectful. What rhymes with 'wackaddoodles?'

JESSICA. I'll go with you, Mr. President.

CRENSHAW. No. I'm great at memorial services. I've never had one corpse walk out on me. You two stay and set up the second act. (as he exits) Wackadoodle…smack a poodle… crap a noodle…

(Jessica & Jorden share a look of pure anguish.)

JESSICA. Jorden…

JORDEN. I know.

JESSICA. He's been president less than an hour, and already he's alienated Congress, blown up the Joint Chiefs. And kick-started two scandals!

JORDEN. I know. I know.

JESSICA. I sure could use some of your wide-eyed optimism about now.

JORDEN. I'm not sure I have any left… *(Singing.)*

THIS IS WHERE IT ENDS
ALL MY DREAMS ARE SHATTERED
WE'VE BEEN DUPED WE DIDN'T THINK
OUR LEADERS LET US DOWN
THIS IS WHERE IT ENDS
THE PRESIDENT'S A MADMAN
OUR COUNTRY'S ON THE BRINK
HE'LL RUN IT IN THE GROUND

JESSICA

THIS IS WHERE IT ENDS
IDEALS NO LONGER MATTER
NOBILITY'S A JOKE
WHEN CROOKS AND FOOLS ABOUND
THIS IS WHERE IT ENDS
THE USA IN TATTERS
WHEN WE ELECT A CLOWN

JORDEN & JESSICA. *(Together.)*

WHEN WE ELECT A CLOWN

(Crenshaw enters with pockets stuffed with cash).

CRENSHAW. Someone call me?

END OF ACT ONE

ACT TWO
Scene 1

AT RISE. INT. OVAL OFFICE - TEN MINUTES LATER
Crenshaw, Jorden and Jessica stand in the same positions as the end of the previous scene.

CRENSHAW. Wow. I must have blacked out for a few minutes... Now, where was I? Oh, yeah. It's my first day in the Oval Office. You are Jessica Woodard, my White Press Secretary, and you're Jorden Fletcher, my Chief of Protocol. I'm meeting the members of my cabinet. I'm in love with a milk lobbyist named Mae Waist, and the Joint Chiefs of Staff just blew themselves up. *(To audience.)* That should help any of you with short term memory problems. *(To Jorden and Jessica.)* Now, have you two figured out a way I can make some fast money outa this presidential gig?

JESSICA. Mr. President. May I remind you that each of your actions has a direct consequence on virtually every citizen in the US?

CRENSHAW. You mean if I drop my pants, the people in Poughkeepsie will feel the breeze?

JESSICA. That's not what I meant, sir. I urge you to take your responsibilities more seriously.

CRENSHAW. Relax, you two. The voters of this country elected me to pretend I'm dealing with their problems, not to take them seriously. Do you think some of my predecessors would have lived in this house if people really wanted the best person for the job?

JESSICA. He does have a point there.

CRENSHAW. We don't elect Einsteins or Ghandis, or even Teddy Roosevelts anymore. Modern democracy is a reality show, and Americans are The Biggest Losers.

JORDEN. That may be true, sir. But there is a certain honor associated with the presidency of the United States.

CRENSHAW. Honor? You want to talk about honor? *(Leaps on desk.)* On the day I was born, the doctor turned me over and slapped my naked butt. So, I challenged him to a duel. That's honor! When I was kicked out of third grade for peeking up the teacher's dress, I refused to tell the other kids she was wearing pink satin panties. That's honor! And when I found a lost wallet on the sidewalk with four hundred dollars cash, I made a point of returning the driver's license. If that's not honor, what is it?!

JORDEN. Easy money?

CRENSHAW. Now you're talking, Fletcher.

(Crenshaw leaps off the table and begins a sprightly song in the Gilbert & Sullivan tradition.)

CRENSHAW. *(Singing.)*

OH, THE LIFE OF A POLITICIAN IS THE LIFE FOR ME.
WHERE I CAN GET PAID FOR HYPERBOLE.
OH, THE LIFE OF A POLITICIAN IS THE LIFE FOR ME.
I LOVE GETTING PAID FOR HYPERBOLE.

WE GET JUNKETS, GIFTS AND LIMOS
AND MANY FANCY PERKS
WITH SPIN DOCTORS TO COVER
WHEN WE ACT LIKE JERKS
WE GET FREE HAIRCUTS, MEALS
AND EVEN POSTAGE TOO
THEN MAKE OURSELVES EXEMPT
FROM THE LAWS WE PASS FOR YOU.

JORDEN & JESSICA. *(Singing.)*

THEY MAKE THEMSELVES EXEMPT FROM
LAWS THEY PASS FOR YOU.

CRENSHAW. *(Singing.)*

YES, THE LIFE OF A POLITICIAN IS THE LIFE FOR ME.
'CAUSE I'D RATHER HAVE MY MONEY THAN MY DIGNITY.

JORDEN & JESSICA. *(Singing.)*

HE'D RATHER HAVE HIS MONEY THAN HIS DIGNITY.

CRENSHAW. *(Singing.)*

THERE ARE SCANDALS, DEALS, AND KICKBACKS
AND LOTS OF POWER GRABS
WE CAN ALWAYS COUNT ON VOTERS
TO PICK UP THE TABS
I'VE ASSISTANTS, PAGES, LOBBYISTS
AND A STAFF OF TWELVE
WHO GLADLY DO THE WORK
WHILE I ENRICH MYSELF

JORDEN & JESSICA. *(Singing.)*

THEY'LL GLADLY DO THE WORK
WHILE HE'LL ENRICH HIMSELF

CRENSHAW. *(Singing.)*

YES, THE LIFE OF A POLITICIAN IS THE LIFE FOR ME
AND I KNOW YOU'LL RE-ELECT US FOR ETERNITY
BUT YOU'RE ONLY GETTING EVERYTHING
THAT YOU DESERVE
'CAUSE SOMEHOW YOU FORGOT THAT
WE WERE MEANT TO SERVE.

JORDEN & JESSICA. *(Singing.)*

'CAUSE SOMEHOW THEY FORGOT THAT
THEY WERE MEANT TO SERVE.

CRENSHAW. *(Singing.)*

OH, THE LIFE OF A POLITICIAN IS THE LIFE FOR ME
'CAUSE I'D RATHER HAVE MY MONEY THAN MY DIGNITY.
YES, THE LIFE OF A POLITICIAN IS THE LIFE FORRRR MEEEEEE!
'CAUSE I'D RATHER HAVE MY MONEY THAN MY DIGNITY.

JORDEN & JESSICA. *(Singing.)*

HE'D RATHER HAVE HIS MONEY THAN HIS DIGNITY.

(Jessica & Jorden shake their heads in disbelief, as Crenshaw finishes with a comic dance step.)

CRENSHAW. Stick with me, Fletcher. And I'll make a politician of you yet.

JORDEN. Sorry. Not interested.

CRENSHAW. A man of integrity, huh? You should hold onto this one, Woodard.

JESSICA. I have no intention of 'holding on' to anyone, sir. And if I may be blunt, if you wish to hold onto this office, I suggest we get down to business.

CRENSHAW. Monkey business? I'm ape if you are. You could be the gorilla my dreams.

JESSICA. Mr. President, I'm trying desperately to hold my patience here!

CRENSHAW. I knew an overly affectionate doctor who was always trying to hold his patients. Oh, wait... That was me. *(Pulls a stethoscope out of his pocket.)* Now tell me where it hurts...

JESSICA. Sir, the people of this country elected you because they believed you could do something positive!

CRENSHAW. Lighten up, Woodard. I've got four years before they wise up.

JESSICA. That's a real comfort, Mr. President.

(Seeing how angry Jessica is, Jorden tries to ease the situation.)

JORDEN. You'll have to excuse Miss Woodard's passion, sir. I assure you, she has only your best interest at heart... and the best interest of our country.

CRENSHAW. Well, as long as the two don't conflict.

(Jessica throws herself down on the chair, Stage Left.)

JORDEN. I believe it's time we focused on your agenda...

CRENSHAW. Last time I checked, my 'genda' was male. *(Checks his pants.)* Yup. That's male all right.

JORDEN. I meant your schedule, sir. As you requested, I set up an appointment with Mr. Fielding, the Director of the Environmental Protection Agency. He should be here shortly.

CRENSHAW. Mr. Fielding? You mean W. Z.?

JORDEN. Yes, sir.

CRENSHAW. Good, old Bill. Send him in as soon as he arrives.

JORDEN. Yes, sir. And the Secretary of State needs to see you about your upcoming international trip.

CRENSHAW. I'm being deported?

JORDEN. No, sir. You have a diplomatic mission coming up. Visiting foreign heads of state.

CRENSHAW. Foreign heads? Who's going to visit the rest of them? Will I get a chance to see Marie Antoinette?

JORDEN. Uh... I'll leave it to Secretary of State Cabot to explain the details.

(Jorden crosses to leave. Jessica rises from the sofa.)

JESSICA. If you're finished with me, sir…

CRENSHAW. I'm finished. *(Batting his eyebrows.)* Was it good for you, too?

(Jessica storms out, Stage Right.)

CRENSHAW. *(CONT'D)* Oh, and Jorden....

JORDEN. Yes, sir?

CRENSHAW. What's the story on Miss Woodard? You think a beautiful, intelligent woman like her could ever fall for a beautiful and intelligent president like me?

JORDEN. Honestly?

CRENSHAW. That's a question you never hear in Washington... but what the heck.

JORDEN. I doubt it, sir. Jessica Woodard is a truly exceptional human being. In the ten years I have had the extreme pleasure of knowing her, she has proven herself to be one of the most talented, forthright, innovative, dedicated, loyal...

CRENSHAW. And her bazoombas ain't bad either.

JORDEN. With all due respect, sir. If you talk like that about Ms. Woodard again, I'm going to punch you in the nose!

CRENSHAW. You can't do that! This is the number one nose in the country. E Proboscis Unum...

JORDEN. I...I'm sorry, sir. I...I don't know what came over me...

CRENSHAW. I do. You're in love with Jessica.

JORDEN. I beg your pardon?

CRENSHAW. You and Jessica. The ingénues of 1600 Pennsylvania Avenue. Passion on the Potomac. Obsession in the Oval Office. Ecstasy in the Executive Branch. You two could make a Kennedy blush.

JORDEN. Believe me, Mr. President. My feelings for Jessica...I mean, Ms. Woodard only extend to the professional...

CRENSHAW. And I'm a member of the Swedish bikini team. *(With an exaggerated accent.)* Yoooo vant I shooood tell her for youooo?

JORDEN. No! I mean...what would she say if she found out?

CRENSHAW. It's been my experience that when confronted with the sudden revelation of love, women will either kiss you passionately, or cough up a hairball. Remind me to show you my hairball collection sometime. It's quite impressive.

JORDEN. May I ask you a personal question, sir?

CRENSHAW. I have absolutely no idea how those sheep got into the Washington Monument! And I'll testify under oath that nobody saw me do it!

JORDEN. What sheep?

CRENSHAW. Never mind. What did you want to ask?

JORDEN. It's about Ms. Woodard...Jessica...

CRENSHAW. Ask away, Fletcher. You're consulting the Einstein of Emotion. The Freud of Fraternization. The Steve Jobs of Jugs. The Bill Gates of Gushiness. The Elon Musk of Lust...

JORDEN. I just want to know if my feelings for Miss Woodard…such as they are...are that obvious?

CRENSHAW. You'd have better luck hiding a donut from a policeman.

JORDEN. I've worked side-by-side with Jessica for ten years. Every time she'd take a new position, I made sure I got transferred to the same place. I sacrificed my own advancement...just to be able to see her every day.

CRENSHAW. And you never told her how you felt?

JORDEN. I could never find the right moment. After a while, all those missed opportunities start to pile up. An inertia of honesty. A big fat dump truck of hesitation...or maybe just a lack of guts.

CRENSHAW. So, tell her. What have you got to lose? Except maybe your dignity. But hey, we're in Washington, so who'd notice?

JORDEN. Maybe after things settle down a bit...

CRENSHAW. Don't con a con man, Fletcher. If you're waiting for a gold-plated moment, go propose to the Sergeant at Fort Knox. It's just a case of gold feet. So, drop the bullion, if you carat all.

JORDEN. That's what I'm afraid of. If I don't time it right, she'll just make a joke out of it. Her speechwriter side will take over and she'll say something way too clever...or too painful.

CRENSHAW. There's something you have to learn about women, Fletcher. Deep down inside is their intestines. And deep down inside that is... Well, it's not a pretty picture. The point is you have to be popcorn.

JORDEN. Popcorn, sir?

CRENSHAW. You ever see unpopped popcorn? It's all these little hard shells that annoy people. Stick in your teeth and hurt your gums. But when you get them near a flame, they burst open. Their inner side is revealed, and that wonderful scent of anticipation fills the air. By exposing their soft inner core, they become irresistible to women... especially in a dark movie theater.

JORDEN. So, you're telling me the secret of romance is to behave like exploding snack food?

CRENSHAW. Drop the hard shell. Turn up the heat. Let your soft insides burst out. She'll either love you...or eat your heart out.

JORDEN. Be popcorn?

CRENSHAW. Be popcorn.

JORDEN. I guess it's worth a try. Do you think there's any chance Jessica could feel the same way?

CRENSHAW. I don't see why not. You're handsome, intelligent, sophisticated. Wait... that makes you practically me.

JORDEN. I wish I had your ability with women, sir.

CRENSHAW. All it takes is equal amounts of confidence, charm and terror.

JORDEN. If you don't mind my asking, Mr. President... Have you ever been in love?

CRENSHAW. Does Congress spend money they don't have? There have been many women in my life, but only one true love... Her name was Dell...

JORDEN. Dell? Where did you meet her, if I may ask?

CRENSHAW. She was a mail order bride. A real piece of work.

JORDEN. Was she beautiful?

CRENSHAW. She was built, I'll say that for her.

JORDEN. Where is she now, Mister President?

CRENSHAW. On my desk.

JORDEN. On your desk?

(He walks over and gestures to the computer on his desk.)

CRENSHAW. Jorden...meet Dell.

JORDEN. Your computer?

"I'M IN LOVE WITH MY PC"

CRENSHAW. *(Singing.)*

I TURN HER ON, SHE WINKS AT ME.
SHE MAKES EVERYTHING RIGHT
I KNOW I'M IN HER MEMORY
WHEN SHE TEMPTS ME WITH HER LOVE BYTE
THEY SAY YOU CAN'T LOVE A MACHINE
SHE'S JUST METAL, WIRES AND PLEXY.
BUT MY LOVE IS NOTHING OBSCENE.
SHE'S JUST PROGRAMMED TO BE SEXY!

I'M IN LOVE WITH MY PC
MY COMPUTER LIKE NO OTHER
I CAN INPUT WHEN I PLEASE
KNOWING SHE WON'T OUTPUT FOR ANOTHER.
SHE KNOWS THE TIGRIS AND EUPHRATES
CAN TELL COUPONS FROM KUWAITIS
WHAT DO I NEED WITH OTHER LADIES?
SHE'S MY MAIN FRAME, CAN'T YOU SEE?
I'M IN LOVE WITH MY PC.

CRENSHAW. *(Singing.)*

SHE NEVER CALLS MY DATA BASE
I CAN ALWAYS SPEAK HER LANGUAGE
ALTHOUGH SHE DOESN'T HAVE A FACE
IN HER SPREADSHEET I CAN LANGUISH.
SHE'S THE APPLE OF MY EYE
THE FLASH IN MY HARD DRIVE
I GIGGLE WHEN SHE GOOGLES
AND DREAM OF STREAMING LIVE

I'M IN LOVE WITH MY PC
MY COMPUTER LIKE NO OTHER
I CAN INPUT WHEN I PLEASE
KNOWING SHE WON'T OUTPUT FOR ANOTHER

SO WHAT IF I DON'T KNOW RAM FROM ROM?
CAN NEVER TAKE HER TO THE PROM?
I ALWAYS KNOW WHERE SHE'S COMING FROM
SHE 'BOOTS UP' JUST FOR ME
I'M IN LOVE WITH MY PC.

THEY SAY SOFTWARE'S NEVER SENSUAL
LET THEM TALK, I WONT LISTEN
'TILL THEY'VE HANDLED HER PERIPHERALS
AND SEEN HOW HER HARDWARE GLISTENS

AND SO I HOPE THAT YOU DON'T MIND
MY TALE OF LOVE ROBOTIC
SOMETIMES LOVE'S NOT ONLY BLIND
IN MY CASE, IT'S PSYCHOTIC

(He ends the song with a leap toward the desk and a kiss on his computer.)

CRENSHAW. It's all about compatibility, Fletcher.

JORDEN. I'm uh, happy for you, Mr. President. However, returning to some semblance of sanity...I'm not sure I can tell Jessica how I feel. After all these years of working beside her. I wouldn't know how to broach the subject.

CRENSHAW. Just leave it to me. If there's one thing I know, it's amore. In fact, I once wrestled 'a moray' eel in my pajamas...but that's another story.

(A KNOCK.)

CRENSHAW. He's back for a rematch!

JORDEN. I believe that's your next appointment. The Secretary of State.

(Jorden crosses Stage Right to open the door. Jessica and JUDD CABOT, 50, enters. He resembles Bud Abbot from the 1940's comedy duo, Abbot & Costello enter.)

JESSICA. Mr. President... May I present Secretary of State Judd Cabot.

CABOT. A pleasure to meet you, Mr. President.

(Cabot crosses to shake hands with Crenshaw. Jorden, looking more than a little moonstruck, crosses over to Jessica's side.)

JESSICA. What's wrong with you?

JORDEN. Nothing. Um...do you like popcorn?

JESSICA. What?

JORDEN. Never mind…

(Jessica & Jorden exit, Stage Right.)

CRENSHAW. So, you're the Secretary of State, eh? Do you take dictation?

CABOT. No, sir.

CRENSHAW. That's okay. I'm not much of a dictator. Although the idea does intrigue me.

CABOT. Mr. President, as Secretary of State my role is to establish your credibility with world leaders.

CRENSHAW. Boy, do you have a job ahead of you.

CABOT. The Undersecretary and I have booked you on an international tour of diplomacy.

CRENSHAW. One day in the White House and they're already telling me to get out of town. By the way, where is the Undersecretary?

CABOT. He should be here any minute. He's trying to get you frequent flyer miles.

CRENSHAW. Great. But I don't want to fly Transvestite Airlines. You wouldn't believe how long it takes to change planes.

ODDFELLOW. He-ey-eyy, Cabot!!

(The door opens Stage Left and LOU ODDFELLOW enters. He is 50 and stocky, looking like Lou Costello from that classic 1940's comedy duo, Abbott & Costello.)

CABOT. There you are, Oddfellow. You know it's not polite to keep the President waiting.

ODDFELLOW. Sorry. I had to help the Secretary of Transportation change a flat.

CABOT. Did you check the President's itinerary?

ODDFELLOW. No, but I got his schedule for the trip.

CRENSHAW. That'll have to do.

ODDFELLOW. (Looking at papers.) This thing really confuses me, Cabot.

CABOT. What's so confusing? For this diplomatic mission, the President flies to seven foreign countries and meets seven foreign leaders. It couldn't be easier.

ODDFELLOW. Yeah. But I keep getting all those foreign leaders names mixed up.

CABOT. It's easy. His first stop is in South Korea, where he meets with President Hoo Yu Meen. Then he flies to New Zealand for discussions with Prime Minister Robert Watt. The next stop is Japan, for a summit with Foreign Minister Aye Donno. Followed by a trip to China, for trade talks with the Chinese Deputy Premier Hees Sum Guy.

ODDFELLOW. *(Confused)* Uh-huh…

CABOT. Then it's onto Germany to meet with Franz Gesundheit. A side trip to Russia to negotiate with Trade Minister Nokitov. His last stop is in London to discuss policy with Deputy Minister Edmond Wright. You see how easy it is?

ODDFELLOW. Let me get this straight... Who's the guy in South Korea?

CABOT. Yes.

ODDFELLOW. Who?

CABOT. That's what I said.

ODDFELLOW. You said who?

CABOT. Hoo Yu Meen.

ODDFELLOW. The guy in South Korea.

CABOT. Yes.

ODDFELLOW. What's his name?

CABOT. No. Watt's the guy in New Zealand.

ODDFELLOW. I'm not talking about New Zealand. I'm talking about South Korea. Who's the leader of South Korea?

CABOT. Exactly.

ODDFELLOW. What?

CABOT. Watt's in New Zealand.

ODDFELLOW. I dunno.

CABOT. Japan.

ODDFELLOW. Let's start again. I want to know the name of the President of South Korea.

CABOT. Hoo.

ODDFELLOW. The President of South Korea.

CABOT. Hoo Yu Meen.

ODDFELLOW. I dunno. He's some guy.

CABOT. No. Sum Guy's in China.

ODDFELLOW. How'd we get to China? I wanna be in Korea!

CABOT. Fine. So, what's your question?

ODDFELLOW. Let me put it this way. If I went to South Korea, they'd tell me who was in charge.

CABOT. At least until the next election.

ODDFELLOW. What?

CABOT. He's in New Zealand.

ODDFELLOW. Knock it off!

CABOT. You have to go to Russia to see him.

ODDFELLOW. Who?

CABOT. I told you. He's in South Korea.

ODDFELLOW. South Korea?

CABOT. Right.

ODDFELLOW. Wright's in South Korea?

CABOT. No. Wright's in London.

ODDFELLOW. What?

CABOT. Watt's in New Zealand.

ODDFELLOW. How should I know?! I'm asking you!

CABOT. And I'm telling you! Watt's in New Zealand.

ODDFELLOW. I dunno!

CABOT. Japan.

ODDFELLOW. Okay. Let's forget Korea. I want to fly to Germany and see the foreign minister. What's his name?

CABOT. No. Watt's in New Zealand.

ODDFELLOW. I'm back in New Zealand! I want to be in Germany! Just tell me the German guy's name.

CABOT. Gesundheit.

ODDFELLOW. I didn't sneeze.

CABOT. I didn't say you did.

ODDFELLOW. Then tell me the name of the guy in Germany.

CABOT. Gesundheit.

ODDFELLOW. Knock it off!

CABOT. That's Russia.

ODDFELLOW. What's in Russia?

CABOT. No. Watt's in New Zealand!

ODDFELLOW. I dunno!

CABOT & ODDFELLOW. *(Together)* Japan!

ODDFELLOW. Okay. Let's forget Germany. Let's say I go to China to meet the Premier...

CABOT. Hees Sum Guy.

ODDFELLOW. Right.

CABOT. You're getting confused again. Wright's in London.

ODDFELLOW. What?

CABOT. Watt's in New Zealand.

ODDFELLOW. How the heck am I supposed to know?! I'm still trying to meet with the Chinese Premier.

CABOT. Hees Sum Guy.

ODDFELLOW. Who?

CABOT. I keep telling you. Hoo's in South Korea.

ODDFELLOW. Who?

CABOT. Now you got it.

ODDFELLOW. Got what?

CABOT. The guy in South Korea.

ODDFELLOW. Who?

CABOT. Exactly.

ODDFELLOW. Who's the guy in South Korea?

CABOT. Has been for years.

ODDFELLOW. Who you mean?

CABOT. That's right.

ODDFELLOW. I thought that was the guy in London?

CABOT. He is.

ODDFELLOW. Who is?

CABOT. Wright is.

ODDFELLOW. Wright is what?

CABOT. Of course not. They're two different people.

ODDFELLOW. Who is two different people?

CABOT. Don't be silly. How could he be?

ODDFELLOW. I dunno!

CABOT & ODDFELLOW. *(Together)* Japan!

ODDFELLOW. Knock it off!

CABOT. He's in Russia.

ODDFELLOW. What's in Russia?

CABOT. Watt's in New Zealand.

ODDFELLOW. Kangaroos! But the President isn't gonna sit down and meet with them!

CABOT. What are you talking about?

ODDFELLOW. Just tell me this... If I go meet the leader of Germany, I say, "Good Morning, Mr...?"

CABOT. Gesundheit.

ODDFELLOW. Why? Did he sneeze?

CABOT. Who?

ODDFELLOW. The guy in Germany!

CABOT. Gesundheit!

ODDFELLOW. Knock it off!

CABOT. He's in Russia!

ODDFELLOW. Who's in Russia?

CABOT. Not unless they have a summit.

ODDFELLOW. What?

CABOT. Watt's in New Zealand!

ODDFELLOW. I dunno!

CABOT, ODDFELLOW & CRENSHAW. *(Together)* Japan!

CABOT. Got it straight now?

ODDFELLOW. *(Frustrated.)* I think so... I go to South Korea and I see who. What's the name of the guy in New Zealand? I dunno, but he's in Japan. I get to China and meet some guy. After that I fly to Germany. I ask the name of the man I'm supposed to talk to, and everybody says 'Gesundheit'. Knock it off, I say, but for that I have to go to Russia. Finally, I end up in London and when I'm there it's all right!

CABOT. See? It couldn't be simpler.

ODDFELLOW. I'm having a ba-a-a-ad day.

CRENSHAW. Maybe I can help... Get the hell out of my office!!!

CABOT. Why?

CRENSHAW. No, that's the building down the street. They have a gym and workout facilities.

ODDFELLOW. What?

CABOT. He's in New Zealand.

ODDFELLOW. Who's in New Zealand?

CABOT. No. Watt's in New Zealand.

ODDFELLOW. I dunno!

CABOT & ODDFELLOW. *(Together)* Japan!!

(They exit, bickering.)

CRENSHAW. *(To audience.)* Have you ever wondered what people in Washington would do if they ever had to get real jobs? *(Picks up the phone.)* Yes. Hello. This is the President. I know, it takes a little getting used to for me, too... I'd like you to schedule an appointment with Miss Waist, the milk lobbyist. That's right. That's her... The one with the big... personality… As soon as possible. Thank you.

(Crenshaw hangs up, just as Mae Waist enters Stage Right.)

CRENSHAW. What kept you?

MAE WAIST. I was being frisked by three burly men with the TSA.

CRENSHAW. I didn't order them to frisk you.

MAE WAIST. I did. Ooooh.

(She sits on the sofa. Crenshaw moves to her side.)

CRENSHAW. So, Mae. May I call you 'Mae?'

MAE WAIST. Call me whatever you like, Mr. President. Just make sure you call me.

CRENSHAW. Growl…And you can call me your little 'boy toy.' *(Leaps onto her lap.)* If you feel yourself getting carried away, just let me know.

MAE WAIST. I'll send you a postcard.

CRENSHAW. Ahhh, my sweetbread. Has anyone ever told you that you're as sensuous as a Jello-filled Jacuzzi?

MAE WAIST. Sure.

CRENSHAW. Really?

MAE WAIST. Of course, I was in a Jacuzzi filled with Jello at the time. I hear it's still wriggling.

CRENSHAW. Oh...You're good.

MAE WAIST. When I'm good, I'm very, very good. And when I'm bad, I'm better.

CRENSHAW. And when you're bad, I'm butter.

MAE WAIST. Then come melt on over here, big boy.

"LOVE AT FIRST GROPE"

MAE WAIST. *(Singing.)*

CAN I HAVE YOUR EAR, MR. PRESIDENT?
YOUR CUTE LITTLE EAR, MR. PRESIDENT?
IT'S SO HARD NOT TO NIBBLE AND COO

CRENSHAW. *(Singing.)*

PLEASE DO!

MAE WAIST. *(Singing.)*

DON'T TRY TO RESIST, MR. PRESIDENT
THIS LOBBYIST AIN'T NEVER BEEN KISSED
MR. PRESIDENT
WELL, THAT MIGHT BE SLIGHTLY UNTRUE…

CRENSHAW. *(Singing.)*

YOU'RE THE ONLY WOMAN
IN THIS ROOM FOR ME
THE LOVE OF MY LIFE
AT LEAST 'TIL TEN AFTER THREE

MAE WAIST. Mind is I adjust the shades?

CRENSHAW. Now that's a lovely view.

MAE WAIST. *(Singing.)*

YOU'RE THE ONE WHO SPARKS MY DESIRE

CRENSHAW. *(Singing.)*

MUST BE MY LOOKS

MAE WAIST. *(Singing.)*

NO. JUST YOUR SIGNATURE I REQUIRE
LOVE AT FIRST GROPE
HOW ILLICITLY FUN!
YOU'RE THE THIRD MAN THIS WEEK
I'VE TOLD HE'S THE ONE

CRENSHAW. *(Singing.)*

LOVE AT FIRST GROPE
SO LOVELY, SO PURE
WELL, I'M NOT SO SURE ABOUT PURE
BUT WHEN YOU THROW ME THOSE CURVES
I CAN HARDLY DEMURE

MAE WAIST. *(Singing.)*
LOVE AT FIRST GROPE
IT TAKES A SPECIAL MAN
TO MAKE ME FEEL THIS WAY
BUT LUCKY FOR YOU

HE'S OUT OF TOWN TODAY

MAE WAIST & CRENSHAW. *(Together.)*

LOVE AT FIRST GROPE
SO EXCITING AND NEW
YOU SCAMMING ME
WHILE I'M CONNING YOU

MAE WAIST & CRENSHAW. *(Together.)*

LOVE AT FIRST GROPE
SO, WHAT IF IT'S NOT REAL

CRENSHAW.
I ACCEPT YOUR OFFER

MAE WAIST & CRENSHAW. *(Together.)*
NOW LET'S CLOSE THIS DEAL

(She kisses him passionately. He staggers to his feet, vainly attempts to smooth down his hair and mustache.)

CRENSHAW. You've done this before, I gather?

MAE WAIST. A lady never tells. And the gentleman are usually too shellshocked to speak.

CRENSHAW. Now that's a purple heart I wouldn't mind getting. So, how's about you and me stepping out for a night of romance?

MAE WAIST. What did you have in mind, Mr. President? As if I don't know.

CRENSHAW. Oh, I don't know… A Day At The Races. A Night At The Opera. A visit to Horsefeathers restaurant for The Coconuts or Duck Soup.

MAE WAIST. Are you asking me out, or reciting your resume?

CRENSHAW. Why don't I slip into something more comfortable? How about you?

MAE WAIST. I'm comfortable.

CRENSHAW. Then why don't I slip into you?

MAE WAIST. Go freshen up, Mr. President. I'll wait right here. I'm pretty fresh already.

CRENSHAW. Whatever you say, my little passion-pot. (*To audience.*) Gotta love executive privilege!

(Crenshaw dashes off, Stage Left. Mae stands, looks up to the portrait of George Washington.)

MAE WAIST. If you were alive, Georgie-boy, I'd set those wooden teeth on fire.

(Jorden enters, Stage Right. He is clearly surprised to find Mae Waist alone in the Oval Office.)

JORDEN. Miss Waist, what are you doing here?

MAE WAIST. Waiting for you, Mr. Fletcher.

(She crosses to him and starts playing with the lapels on his jacket. Jorden is thrilled and petrified by her aggressiveness.)

JORDEN. Where...where's the President?

MAE WAIST. He's making himself presentable. That should give us at least a month. Has anyone ever told you you're as sensuous as a Jacuzzi filled with Jello?

JORDEN. Ulp... no.

MAE WAIST. Then do I have plans for you, mister…

(Jorden slips away, but Mae continues to chase him around the office.)

JORDEN. Ms. Waist. This is the Oval Office! It deserves some respect.

MAE WAIST. Tell that to Monica Lewinski. If you touch me in the right spot, I'll sing the Star-Spangled Banner.

JORDEN. The President could come back at any moment!

MAE WAIST. That would be inconvenient.

JORDEN. I'm in love with another woman!

MAE WAIST. Yeah? Has she ever kissed you like this?

(Mae grabs him and kisses him passionately. After a moment, she lets him come up for air.)

JORDEN. *(Dazed.)* uh... um... not really...

MAE WAIST. How about like this?

(Another kiss, even more passionate than the first.)

JORDEN. *(Even more dazed.)* uh... um... definitely not....

MAE WAIST. Then I'm sure she never kissed you like this...

(She bends Jorden back over the desk and smothers him with a kiss so passionate, the entire audience will be tempted to blush. Suddenly, Jessica appears at the door, Stage Right.)

JESSICA. Jorden!

JORDEN. *(Leaping up.)* Jessica!

JESSICA. What are you doing?! No, don't answer that!

MAE WAIST. So, is this the woman you said can't kiss like I do?

JESSICA. You said that…?

JORDEN. Uh, yes. I mean no! I mean, that is none of your business, Ms. Waist. And I would appreciate you not interfering in my personal affairs!

MAE WAIST. I thought I was your personal affair, Mr. Fletcher.

JESSICA. Jorden!

JORDEN. Ms. Waist!

(Crenshaw enters from Stage Left, wearing a ridiculous paisley bathrobe, an ascot tied around his neck, and brown support socks on his otherwise bare legs.)

CRENSHAW. Oh, Maaaae! Your boy toy is back!

Notices the angry expressions all around him.

CRENSHAW. *(CONT'D)* Did I miss something?

(Mae crosses to Crenshaw and wraps her arm in his.)

MAE WAIST. Not at all, Mr. President. Mr. Fletcher just suggested you and I take a walk in the West Wing.

CRENSHAW. Good idea, Fletcher. You two carry on.

JESSICA. As if!!

CRENSHAW. Come along, Ms. Waist. Have I ever showed you my hairball collection? It's really quite impressive.

MAE WAIST. Oooh. I'd like to come up and see it some time.

(Mae & Crenshaw exit, Stage Left. Jorden is left on stage with a furious Jessica.)

JORDEN. Jessica. I know that may have looked bad, but it was really just...

JESSICA. You don't have to say anything, Jorden. We're co-workers. Nothing more. I have no right to judge you and your hopelessly narcissistic, predictably adolescent male behavior!

JORDEN. I don't want to be just your co-worker! I want more. I love you.

JESSICA. And when did you come to that conclusion? When you were playing tonsil hockey with that oversexed lobbyist?!

JORDEN. Damn it, Jessica... I have always loved you! Why do you think I followed you from job to job? Why do you think I gave up everything so I could stay by your side?

JESSICA. I never asked you to!

JORDEN. That's right. You never asked. You never asked me to do, or to be anything at all! You won't let any feelings mess up your perfect agenda, could you?

JESSICA. I'm perfectly happy with my life, Jorden. I don't need to make apologies to you or any other man.

JORDEN. You never make apologies. You never make promises. In the past ten years, you have never given me the slightest indication you felt anything for me at all!

JESSICA. Let me get this straight… I find you wriggling on the desk of the President of the United States, swallowing the face of that woman, and suddenly, it's my behavior that's in question?!

JORDEN. Jessica. I'm sorry. I should have let you know how I felt years ago. That's what the President told me to...

JESSICA. Back that truck up! You told that...lunatic you've known for two hours what you couldn't tell me in ten years of us working together?!

JORDEN. Yes, but...you see...

JESSICA. Mr. Fletcher. I have had quite enough of this conversation.

JORDEN. Jessica, please. We can get past this!

JESSICA. There's nothing to get past, Jorden. *(Icily.)* There never was.

JORDEN. Jessica…?

JESSICA. Let me be clear, Mr. Fletcher… There never was.

(Jessica stares at him with defiance masking her pain. Jorden stares back with anger and hurt.)

JORDEN. Maybe there never was anything for you, Jessica. But there has never been anything else for me. At least I'm not afraid to admit it.

(He exits, Stage Right. Pops his head back in seconds later.)

JORDEN. (CONT'D) Well, I mean admit it now… Since I just told you and everything… and… (Giving up.) uh…Goodbye, Jessica…

(He ducks back out again. Jessica is left alone on stage. A soft melody begins to rise. The lights dim and she stands in the glare of a single spotlight. Her voice is laced with doubt and vulnerability.)

"QUESTIONS"

JESSICA. *(Singing.)*

WHO COULD HAVE KNOWN
WHAT WAS TO BE?
HOW DID I MISS
WHAT HAPPENED TO ME?

WHERE DID IT START?
WHEN DID I FALL?
WHY DID MY HEART
PUT ME THROUGH IT ALL?

I THOUGHT THAT I KNEW ALL OF THE ANSWERS
THOUGHT I HAD EVERYTHING PLANNED
I WOULD NEVER BE ONE OF THOSE DANCERS
WHO WOULD FOLLOW THE MOVES OF A MAN

BUT SOMEHOW IT CHANGED
WHEN, I CAN'T SAY
I LET SOMEONE IN
THEN SOMEONE WENT AWAY
WHY DIDN'T I KNOW
HOW IT WOULD BE?
WAS I SO BLIND?
WHY COULDN'T I SEE?

THERE'S CRUELTY INHERENT IN QUESTIONS
A RAZOR DISGUISED IN THE DOUBT
THE WORST PART ABOUT INTROSPECTION
IS THE ANSWERS YOU WON'T LET SLIP OUT

NOW WHAT CAN I DO?
WHERE CAN I GO?
WHO CAN I TRUST?
HOW WILL I KNOW?

JESSICA. *(Singing.)*

I WAS THE PERSON WHO HAD ALL THE ANSWERS
THE WOMAN ALWAYS IN CONTROL
I LAUGHED AT THE 'LEAVE-IT-TO-CHANCERS'
I TRIED TO PRETEND I WAS WHOLE

BUT SOMEHOW IT CHANGED
WHEN, I CAN'T SAY
I LET SOMEONE IN
THEN SOMEONE WENT AWAY

HOW WILL IT BE?
WHEN I DECIDE
TO FINALLY LET OUT
ALL I'M HOLDING INSIDE

I KNOW I'LL GET THROUGH
SOMEHOW, I'LL SURVIVE
UNCOVER THAT PART
OF ME STILL ALIVE

OH, BUT NOT 'TIL THAT DAY
WILL I LET HIM HEAR
THE QUESTIONS THAT HAUNT ME
AND THE ANSWERS I FEAR

(Jessica bows her head and exits, Stage Right. The stage remains dim. After applause, Crenshaw enters from Stage Left. He is fully dressed again, but looking very, very satisfied.)

CRENSHAW. Anybody in here? Uh oh. I sure hope the national debt isn't too high to pay the electric bill.

(He claps his hands twice. Suddenly all the lights come back up full.)

CRENSHAW. *(CONT'D)* Isn't technology wonderful? *(Crosses to his desk.)* Sorry, Dell. I'm going to marry Miss Waist...as soon as I make some real money, that is. She's on her way to Fort Knox right now to pick out a wedding ring. So, it looks like you're obsolete...

CRENSHAW. *(CONT'D)* No, don't monitor me like that and look at me all Google-eyed. It's best this way. After a while, you wouldn't have been turned on by my three-and-a-half-inch floppy. *(To audience.)* What can I say? I'm older than you think. *(Straightens his tie.)* Now, the question it, 'How can I make some big money to support my new wife?' *(Pause, louder.)* I said, 'How can I make some big money to support my new wife?!'

(A KNOCK)

CRENSHAW. *(CONT'D)* Ah! That's my cue!

(The door opens Stage Right, and Jessica enters with the new director of the Environmental Protection Agency... W. Z. FIELDING, 60, looking like 1930's comedian, W.C. Fields.)

JESSICA. Mr. President? Your three o'clock is here.

CRENSHAW. Thank you, Jessica. Your timing is impeccable. But then, I've always considered myself rather 'peccable.'

JESSICA. May I introduce Mr. Fielding. Director of the Environmental Protection Agency.

W. Z. FIELDING. Thank you, my little chickadee. Maybe I could interest you in a little promenade along the Potomac after I drink my lunch. It might make for an interesting diversion. Ye-e-es, indeedy.

JESSICA. Humph. Men!

(Jessica storms out, Stage Right.)

W. Z. FIELDING. Your Press Secretary seems a bit pressed off.

CRENSHAW. Don't mind her. She's on the rebound over me. So Bill, you old horse's ascot. How did you end up in Washington?

W. Z. FIELDING. A curious tale, Mr. President. A curious tale. I was imbibing the spirits of inspiration at my favorite watering hole, when I happened to mention that I knew you. Since I was the only one in town who'd admit to that sordid little detail, they gave me a title and a salary. Director of Environmental Protection. Eight figures, plus expenses.

(He pulls out a bottle in a paper bag. Takes a hefty swig.)

CRENSHAW. What's that?

W. Z. FIELDING. Expenses.

CRENSHAW. I thought you didn't believe in work.

W. Z. FIELDING. They gave me a government job at a ridiculous salary. Nobody said anything about work. Personally, I believe work is a noble institution meant for the less fortunate.

CRENSHAW. Less fortunate?

W. Z. FIELDING. Those afflicted with wives and children.

CRENSHAW. There's a lot of that going around lately.

W. Z. FIELDING. A plague, my good man. A veritable plague.

CRENSHAW. So, you're with the Environmental Protection Agency, eh? I guess that makes sense. Any time I've seen you, you've usually been polluted.

W. Z. FIELDING. Your wit knows no bounds, Mr. President. Of course, it knows no humor either.

CRENSHAW. Oh, yeah? I could outwit you with half my brain tied behind my back!

W. Z. FIELDING. I admit you've always been more of a half-wit than me.

CRENSHAW. Enough chatter, Bill. I have a country to run into the ground. 'Wit' or 'wit-out' you. So, let's get down to business. How can I profit from the EPA? Other than having you declared a toxic dump?

W. Z. FIELDING. It is rather propitious you should ask, Mr. President. Very propitious indeed. I've set the elaborate minutia of my lubricated brain to work on that very problem. And I have devised an answer to your present quandary.

CRENSHAW. Let me guess. You're going to Velcro the hole in the ozone layer?

W. Z. FIELDING. Don't knock ozone depletion. Anything that fries children and dogs can't be all bad. Ye-ees, indeed.

CRENSHAW. So, what is your big idea?

W. Z. FIELDING. A stroke of brilliance, Mr. President. You know about evolution, I presume?

CRENSHAW. Of course. What kind of fool do you take me for?

W. Z. FIELDING. A long-standing one.

CRENSHAW. Thank you.

W. Z. FIELDING. Don't mention it.

CRENSHAW. If I remember correctly, evolution started two hundred years ago, when George Washington helped the British become extinct in North America. They called it the American Evolution. The survival of the fattest...which means you should live forever.

W. Z. FIELDING. Your mental prophylactics amaze even me, Mr. President. Allow me to elucidate... Think of evolution like a giant Fruit of The Loom assembly line, and Mother Nature is Inspector Seventeen. Her job is to look at all the underwear going by and pick out the shorts that don't work right. It's called natural selection. Those that fit snugly survive, and the odd lots become extinct.

CRENSHAW. Like dinosaurs, dodo birds, and lawyers with morals?

W. Z. FIELDING. Precisely. Our job at the EPA is to think we are smarter than Mother Nature and overrule all her decisions. If she decides a species isn't worth surviving, we spend mind-boggling amounts of money to prove her wrong.

CRENSHAW. Why?

W. Z. FIELDING. Years from now, do you want your grandchildren to have to go to a museum to see the world's last pair of defective underwear?

CRENSHAW. Well, when you put it that way...

W. Z. FIELDING. When my department declares a species endangered, we make regulations to protect it.

CRENSHAW. What's a regulation?

W. Z. FIELDING. It's exactly like a law...but isn't.

CRENSHAW. Why don't you just pass laws?

W. Z. FIELDING. We can't. Only the legislative branch can pass a law. It's in the Constitution.

CRENSHAW. So you pass regulations?

W. Z. FIELDING. By the thousands

CRENSHAW. Regulations that are exactly the same as laws?

W. Z. FIELDING. That's right.

CRENSHAW. And nobody gets a chance to vote on them?

W. Z. FIELDING. Correctamundo.

CRENSHAW. And everybody has to follow them, no matter how crazy they may be?

W. Z. FIELDING. They can be arrested or fined if they don't.

CRENSHAW. But they're not actually laws...because Congress didn't pass them.

W. Z. FIELDING. You've summarized the system beautifully. Yes, Indeed.

CRENSHAW. So that whole 'taxation without representation' thing...?

W. Z. FIELDING. ..doesn't apply to anything a random bureaucrat makes up out of thin air or personal agenda. Ain't it delightful?

CRENSHAW. (to audience) Wouldn't ya know? The craziest part of the whole play...and it's all true!

W. Z. FIELDING. Allow me to elucidate...

"REGULATIONS"

W. Z. FIELDING. (Singing.)

BACK IN THE DAY
BOSTON TEA PARTY SAY
COLONISTS RAISED AGITATION
MOTHER ENGLAND INSISTED
AND COLONIES RESISTED
NO TAXATION WITHOUT REPRESENTATION!

FAST FORWARD TO NOW
PLEASE EXPLAIN TO ME HOW
WE'RE BACK IN THE SAME SITUATION
MILLIONS OF RULES
CREATED BY FOOLS
REGULATION IS NOT LEGISLATION!

W. Z. FIELDING & CRENSHAW. (Singing.)

REGULATION
PLEASE DO WHAT WE SAY
REGULATION
OR WE'LL PUT YOU AWAY
IT'S THE LAW OF THE LAND BY DECREE

REGULATION
YET YOU HAVE NO CHOICE
REGULATION
NOT EVEN A VOICE
WE ASSUME THAT'S HOW IT SHOULD BE
THIS PERVERSION OF DEMOCRACY
A BUREACRAT'S WET DREAM, YOU'LL SEE

W. Z. FIELDING & CRENSHAW. (Singing.)

REGULATION
GOT US BY THE BILLS
REGULATION
THEY'RE EXERTING THEIR WILL
OVER EVERY PART OF OUR DAY
REGULATION
SOME BUREAUCRAT TROLL
REGULATION
HAS TAKEN CONTROL
AND NOW HAS THE ULTIMATE SAY
ON WHAT YOU EAT, DRIVE OR PAY
BUT HOW DID IT END UP THIS WAY?
REGULATION INSTEAD OF LEGISLATION.

W. Z. FIELDING. As I was saying, before I was so rudely interrupted by your spontaneous civics lesson... Thanks to this perversion of the Constitution, any government agency can pass whatever rules and regulations we want. And we can even put you in jail if you don't do what we say. When we decide a species is endangered, we pass a regulation to protect it. After that, anyone who threatens the species, gets hit with a heavy fine.

CRENSHAW. Like cutting down trees near a spotted owl.

W. Z. FIELDING. Correctamundo. Let's say, phonetically speaking, we declare a species endangered that people just aren't able to avoid.

CRENSHAW. Like what? Elks? Moose? Shriners?

W. Z. FIELDING. House flies.

CRENSHAW. Flies are an endangered species?

W. Z. FIELDING. It wouldn't be that hard to find a few scientists in need of a generous government grant to back us up on that. We agencies can do amazing things with statistics. A few years ago, we hamstrung an entire city because it endangered a few beetles. Butt-ugly little buggers, too.

CRENSHAW. So, if you pass this house fly law...

W. Z. FIELDING. Correction…this regulation.

CRENSHAW. ...This house fly regulation. Then every time someone swats a fly...

W. Z. FIELDING. ...they have to pay us...let's say, ten thousand dollars. And if anyone tries to build a home within a fly's natural habitat...

CRENSHAW. Which includes all of North America...

W. Z. FIELDING. ...they'd have to pay an even bigger fine!

CRENSHAW. A fly tax? I like it!

W. Z. FIELDING. Let's not use the word 'tax.' We'll call it a "contribution." They always fall for that one.

CRENSHAW. There's a taxpayer born every minute.

W. Z. FIELDING. It's what makes this country great.

CRENSHAW. I can see the billboards now. Save the flies, win valuable prizes. *(Pause.)* Off the record, Bill. Isn't this all a bit...unethical?

W. Z. FIELDING. You cut me to the quick, Mr. President! After all, it depends on your definition of what the word 'is' is...

CRENSHAW. Where have I heard that before?

W. Z. FIELDING. Besides it's only unethical if someone gets caught. Who do you have running the Justice Department?

CRENSHAW. Barney Fife.

W. Z. FIELDING. Then I'd say our ethics are beyond reproach. Yes, Indeedy. Thanks to you, parents a generation from now won't have to explain to their snot-nosed little brats what a fly swatter was used for. Every time they see roadkill swarming with insects, they'll think of you.

CRENSHAW. Really?

W. Z. FIELDING. I know I do... I can have my people draw up the regulations immediately.

CRENSHAW. W. Z., it's a profit doing government with you.

W. Z. FIELDING. The profit is all mine. Yes, indeed.

(He exits, Left. Crenshaw rubs his hands with glee and punches the intercom.)

CRENSHAW. *(Into intercom.)* Jessica, please come in here a moment…

JESSICA. *(Entering.)* Yes, sir?

CRENSHAW. Have you noticed a peculiar lack of flies around here lately?

JESSICA. It's January.

CRENSHAW. So? I'm pretty sure flies don't have calendars. I want you to leak a story to the press that says flies are becoming extinct.

JESSICA. Flies, sir?

CRENSHAW. Blame it on global warming. Or global cooling. Or global something or other.

JESSICA. You must be joking!

CRENSHAW. I don't think so. I usually know when I am.

JESSICA. Does this have anything to do with Mr. Fielding heading the EPA?

CRENSHAW. Stop being so suspicious. I don't have a dishonest bone in my body. Although I wouldn't trust my cartilage as far as I could throw it. If I only knew what my ligaments were up to... They have a tendon to stretch the truth.

JESSICA. Mr. President, as your Press Secretary and official White House Spokesperson, I cannot simply fabricate stories. I do have my ethics.

CRENSHAW. I have ethics, too. But I never allow them to interfere with what I'm about to do. Besides, I'm not asking you to fabricate stories. Just make them up.

"TRUTH IS A RELATIVE THING"

CRENSHAW. *(Singing.)*

TRUTH IS A FUNGIBLE THING
TRUST ME, I KNOW WHAT I SING
JUST YELL 'IT'S FAKE NEWS!'
THEN THEY'LL CHANGE THEIR VIEWS
TRUTH IS A FUNGIBLE THING

FACTS ARE A MESSY AFFAIR
SO, I PULL THEM OUT OF THIN AIR
IT HELPS TO CONFUSE
CLAIM YOU WIN WHEN YOU LOSE
FACTS ARE A MESSY AFFAIR

WHAT'S A LITTLE WHITE LIE,
OR TWITTER WELL-PLACED
IF IT KEEPS VOTERS STILL ON YOUR TEAM?
PROMISES MADE ARE SO OFTEN DELAYED
JUST LEARN NOT TO SAY WHAT YOU MEAN

TRUTH IS A PLIABLE THING
MORE LIKE A BUNGIE CORD SPRING
DON'T FRET OR REGRET, IT'S
MORE FUN WHEN YOU STRETCH IT
DISINFORMATION IS KING

HONESTY IS A RELATIVE THING
WITH AN OFTEN NONSENSICAL RING
SOMETIMES INDEFENSIBLE
OR INCOMPREHENSIBLE
HONESTY'S A RELATIVE THING

CRENSHAW. *(Singing.)*

TRUTH HAS A MALLEABLE SIDE
I DON'T EVEN KNOW WHEN I'VE LIED
A FALSEHOOD FORGIVABLE
MAKES LIFE MORE LIVABLE
TRUTH HAS A MALLEABLE SIDE

WHAT'S A LITTLE WHITE LIE,
OR TWITTER WELL-PLACED
IF IT KEEPS VOTERS STILL ON YOUR TEAM?
PROMISES MADE ARE SO OFTEN DELAYED
JUST LEARN NOT TO SAY WHAT YOU MEAN
AND I NEVER SAY WHAT I MEAN!

JESSICA. Mr. President, I still can't...

CRENSHAW. You know, Fletcher was right. He told me you had the most beautiful eyes he'd ever seen.

JESSICA. *(Stunned.)* Jorden said that?

CRENSHAW. Yes. He babbles for hours about your dazzling intellect and sensuous personality. But says he can't find enough words to describe that mesmerizing sparkle of your eyes.

JESSICA. Mesmerizing sparkle? Stiff, proper Jorden said that?

CRENSHAW. Hard to believe, I know. He kept on about how he can't live without you. That nothing in his life makes any sense without you in it. I've never seen a man so wretchedly in love.

JESSICA. The same Jorden who was kissing that over-sexed lobbyist said that?!

CRENSHAW. He didn't have a choice. I ordered him to warmup her lips for me. And you know Jorden could never refuse anything the President of the United States might ask.

JESSICA. ...he does take his job seriously...

CRENSHAW. Not as seriously as his love for you. I bet right now he's working on another love poem.

JESSICA. *Another* love poem?

CRENSHAW. He has a whole stack of them. That man really has a way with words.

JESSICA. Are we talking about the same Jorden Fletcher here? Brown hair. This tall? Clumsy with women?

CRENSHAW. The man you love.

JESSICA. The man I love?

CRENSHAW. There. Was that so hard to admit?

JESSICA. The man I…love...

CRENSHAW. That's right. The man you love. After all…

"MORE THAN THE SUM OF HIS PARTS"

CRENSHAW. *(Singing.)*

HE'S MORE THAN THE SUM OF HIS PARTS
I HARDLY KNOW WHERE TO START
ALL OF HIS ATTRIBUTES
ARE SO DAMNABLY CUTE
HE'S MORE THAN THE SUM OF HIS PARTS

JESSICA. *(Singing.)*

HE'S MORE THAN THE SUM OF HIS PARTS
WHO CHARMED HIS WAY INTO MY HEART
MAYBE I SHOULD EXPLORE
HOW MUCH I ADORE
HE'S MORE THAN THE SUM OF HIS PARTS

CRENSHAW & JESSICA. *(Singing.)*

SO MUCH MORE THAN THE SUM OF HIS PARTS

CRENSHAW. Now why don't you run along and leak that little fly story for me?

JORDEN. *(Entering.)* Excuse me, Mr. President... Ms. Woodard, you have to prepare for today's press briefing. The reporters are filing in already.

(She looks up at him with an infatuated smile.)

JORDEN. *(CONT'D)* What's the matter with you?

JESSICA. I've suddenly realized… I love popcorn.

JORDEN. Really?

JESSICA. *(Smiling.)* Really.

(They exit happily. Crenshaw runs to the telephone.)

CRENSHAW. *(Into phone.)* Get me CNN. Yes, I'll hold.

(As he waits, he starts singing some inane Muzac song… as if he is performing a duet with the 'hold' music.)

CRENSHAW. *(CONT'D)* Yes. This is a highly reliable source named, oh I don't know...Fred...or Irving, maybe. Okay, that's good, too...You should know about a conspiracy to drive flies into extinction...The FBI is conspiring with corporations that make insect repellent...You think it would make a good news story? Really? I hadn't thought of that...

(Cheato and Hobo dash in from Stage Left. They cower by the door. Crenshaw hangs up the telephone.)

CRENSHAW. *(CONT'D.)* Uh…Gotta go. *(Hangs up.)* Uh…That was a collect call from the Psychic Friends Network. They knew I'd accept the charges.

CHEATO. *(Shrugs.)* Hokay.

(They continue to cower by the door, listening for footsteps.)

CRENSHAW. Hiding from someone?

CHEATO. No. Why you ask?

CRENSHAW. Oh, no reason. Lose something?

CHEATO. No.

HOBO. *(Honking his bicycle horn.)* Honk.

CRENSHAW. Did someone else lose something?

CHEATO. Now thassa possibility.

CRENSHAW. And did the something that someone lost end up in his pocket?

(Hobo sheepishly pulls a watch, two wallets, a necktie, a flimsy nightgown, a pair of candlesticks, and other assorted items from the pockets and lining of his rumpled trenchcoat.)

CHEATO. Funny thing. We can't figure out why people keep shoving stuff inna his pocket like that?

CRENSHAW. Go figure. So, if it isn't Senator Subsidy and the Speaker of the House.

CHEATO. It isn't.

CRENSHAW. Oh, I forgot. You wear many hats.

CHEATO. That'sa right.

(Cheato and Hobo both take off their hats to reveal another smaller one beneath. They remove this second hat to reveal an even tinier one beneath that.)

CRENSHAW. *(To audience.)* And you thought you were in for a night of culture... *(To Cheato.)* So, if you aren't in the Senate or the cabinet, who are you this time? The Atomic Energy Commission?

CHEATO. Naw. I hadda 'fall out' with my boss. He was getting 'critical' and said my desk was a 'mass.' And they were always having me run people around the city. "urunium here, uranium there." Finally, it all blew up in my face.

CRENSHAW. I wouldn't know how to 'reactor' that.

CHEATO. I'm glad that'sa your line.

CRENSHAW. So, what other jobs have you had? Majority whip?

CHEATO. Couldn't afford the black leather boots.

CRENSHAW. Secretary of the Inferior?

CHEATO. They said I wasn't qualified.

CRENSHAW. Secretary of Labor?

CHEATO. Too much work. Besides, after seeing my mom go through labor, no way I'ma gonna do that.

CRENSHAW. Supreme Court Justice?

CHEATO. I heard there wasn't any.

CRENSHAW. Secretary of Comas?

CHEATO. I was asleep when the job was passed out.

CRENSHAW. Well, I'm fresh out of straight lines.

CHEATO. I give you a hint. I pay people not to grow things.

CRENSHAW. Family planning?

CHEATO. Secretary of Agriculture. I pay millionsa to farmers in Nebraska not to grow wheat. I pay millionsa to farmers in Iowa not to grow corn. And I pay millionsa to farmers in Kentucky not to grow tobacco.

CRENSHAW. Getting all those people not to work must be a tough job.

CHEATO. Yeah, but somebody's gotta do it.

CRENSHAW. If you're the Secretary of Agriculture, who's he?

HOBO. *(Honking his bicycle horn.)* Honk.

(Hobo pulls a miniature picket fence on a stick and holds it up by his face.)

CHEATO. Secretary of De Fence.

CRENSHAW. I should have known. So what do I owe the pleasure of your visit this time? And I use 'pleasure' in the complete opposite sense of the word.

CHEATO. *(Trying to be subtle.)* Ohhh... We didn't mean to *bug* you...

CRENSHAW. Really?

HOBO. *(Honking his bicycle horn.)* Honk.

CHEATO. He says he's feeling a bit *swarm*...

CRENSHAW. Does he now?

HOBO. *(Honking his bicycle horn.)* Honk.

CHEATO. He says 'Maybe you better check if your fly is open...'

CRENSHAW. I get the feeling you're trying to tell me something.

CHEATO. Hokay. We know alla 'bout this house fly scam. We thought you'd wanna make us partners in the deal.

CRENSHAW. And why would I do that?

HOBO. *(Honking his bicycle horn.)* Honk. Honk.

CHEATO. His Uncle Wilbur runs a fly farm in Arkansas.

CRENSHAW. How do you breed flies?

CHEATO. The usual. You take 'em out to dinner. A little dancing. Compliment their eyes. They love-a that.

CRENSHAW. I knew there was a little pest in his family.

CHEATO. In a good year, Uncle Wilbur can breed ten or twenny zillion flies on his farm. It'sa gonna be hard to say those little darlings are going extinct with twenny zillion new pesky bambinos buzzing around every year.

HOBO. *(Honking his bicycle horn.)* Honk.

CRENSHAW. And I suppose you happen to have a solution?

CHEATO. Sure, sure. As Secretary of Agriculture, I make sure Uncle Wilbur getsa nice government subsidy not to breed flies.

CRENSHAW. Hmmmm. A subsidy not to breed flies?

CHEATO. We could even puta on a tariff on flies from China.

CRENSHAW. Of course. We have to protect American insects from foreign competition.

CHEATO. If we don't the Japanese, they gonna make 'em faster ana cheaper.

HOBO. *(Honking his bicycle horn.)* Honk.

CRENSHAW. They could corner the annoying insect market. Present company excepted, of course. Uh…you do realize we're talking about billions of dollars with this fly tax?

CHEATO. A billion here, a billion there. Sooner or later, you're talkin' real money.

CRENSHAW. Gentlemen...I think we have a deal.

HOBO. *(Honking his bicycle horn.)* Honk.

(Cheato slaps at his arm.)

CRENSHAW. I believe you owe the government ten thousand dollars.

CHEATO. No. I no think it'sa fly. *(To Hobo.)* That look like a fly to you?

(Hobo looks at the smudge on Cheato's arm. Picks it up with his thumb and forefingers, examines it, then pops it in his mouth. Then nods enthusiastically.)

CHEATO. *(CONT'D)* Damn.

CRENSHAW. About that ten thousand dollar fine...

CHEATO. He ate it. Let him pick up the check.

HOBO. *(Honking his bicycle horn.)* Honk!

CRENSHAW. We'll say that one's on the house. Or at least the Senate. Now help me write my speech for CNN.

CHEATO. Hokay. You got a pen?

CRENSHAW. No. But I'm sure he has.

(Hobo pulls a few pens, one at a time, out of his coat pocket.)

CRENSHAW. *(CONT'D)* Is that all?

Hobo shakes his head and dumps a hundred more on the desk.

CRENSHAW. *(CONT'D)* I'd like to take him with me the next time I go looking for a new car.

(Hobo dumps dozens of car keys out of his pocket.)

CRENSHAW. *(CONT'D)* On top of that, he's stealing the scene. Now, let me think...

(They all pretend to think, in increasingly ridiculous poses. Cheato stands over Crenshaw's shoulder, as he writes furiously.)

CHEATO. Ah ha... Hmmm. Oh, that'sa good... Dot your eyes... Now dot your eyebrows...

CRENSHAW. *(Annoyed)* Do you want to write this?

CHEATO. I no can write.

HOBO. *(Honking his bicycle horn.)* Honk.

CRENSHAW. What did he say?

CHEATO. He said, you spell 'philatelist' wrong.

CRENSHAW. I'm not trying to spell 'philatelist'. I'm trying to spell 'fly.'

HOBO. *(Honking his bicycle horn.)* Honk.

CHEATO. 's okay then.

CRENSHAW. There. All done.

CHEATO. Oh, that'sa good.

CRENSHAW. How do you know?

CHEATO. I said I no can write. I didn't say I no can read.

HOBO. *(Honking his bicycle horn.)* Honk.

CRENSHAW. Everybody's a critic. *(To Intercom.)* Jorden, can you get everyone in here? I want some feedback on my speech before I deliver it to the press.

(Other actors start to enter from both the Stage Left and Stage Right doors. W. Z. Fielding, Mae Waist, Cabot & Oddfellow, The Three Stupids -- their clothes torn, and their faces blackened with soot. Behind all of them enter Jorden and Jessica.

NOTE: If budget and casting allow, other recognizable comedians from the 1920's through 1940's could enter at this point. HAROLD LLOYD, CHARLIE CHAPLIN, LAUREL & HARDY, RED SKELTON, LUCILLE BALL, JIMMY DURANTE, BOB HOPE, BING CROSBY, CARMEN MIRANDA, etc. A potentially humorous argument could break out between the Chaplin look-alike and Hobo, as the two silent comedians attempt to steal each other's wallets with their different styles of pantomime.)

CRENSHAW. *(CONT'D)* Thank you all for coming. I'd like your reaction to my new State Of The Onion Address. I guarantee it will bring tears to your eyes.

(They flank the new president. Hobo flips the wastebasket over and straps it to his chest with a pair of suspenders. From his pocket, he pulls out drumsticks and begins a soft drum roll.)

CRENSHAW. *(CONT'D)* Four snores and seven minutes ago, us foreflushers brought forth upon this continent, a new degradation. Deceived itS citizenry and dangled a proposition that all minds are created equal.

(As he speaks, the others softly begin to hum THE BATTLE HYMN OF THE REPUBLIC. Except, of course, Jorden and Jessica, who are appalled by the spectacle.)

CRENSHAW. *(CONT'D)* Now we have engaged in a great civil wastetocracy, testing whether our nation, or any nation, so deceived and so emasculated, can so much endure.

(The melodic HUMMING grows louder. Hobo executes another flashy drum roll on the wastebasket.)

CRENSHAW. *(CONT'D)* We are muddled in the very heart of that incompetence. But without your apathy…we cannot dominate, we cannot complicate, we cannot mess up your lives. Voters will little note, nor long remember what we say here. But they will spend years paying for what we do here!

(The humming in the background turns into the soft strains of the song's chorus, which flows under Crenshaw's speech.)

CRENSHAW. *(With rising fervor.)* It is a bother for us to be here dedicated to the great tasks remaining before us. But from your paychecks, we demand increased contributions and the last full measure of your earnings.

OTHER COMEDIANS. *(Softly)*

LORDY, HOW WE TRY TO FOOL YA
LORDY, HOW WE TRY TO FOOL YA
LORDY HOW WE TRY TO FOOL YA
OUR SPENDING MARCHES ON...

CRENSHAW. That we highly resolve the budget will not be balanced again! That this nation, under foot, shall be newly bankrupt of freedom. And that a government above the people... that'll lie to the people... yet abhor the people... shall now profit for all we're worth!!

(A loud DRUM ROLL on the wastebasket sets the group marching. As Crenshaw finishes his impassioned speech, the comedians behind him erupt in a new version of The Battle Hymn Of The Republic.)

OTHER COMEDIANS. *(Rising volume.)*

MINE EYES HAVE SEEN THE RAPING
OF U.S. PROSPERITY
WITH THE LAWS AND REGULATIONS
PAID BY YOU, AND NOT BY ME

MORE

OTHER COMEDIANS. *(Rising volume.)*

BUT WE KNOW WE WON'T BE BLAMED
BECAUSE OF VOTER APATHY
OUR SPENDING MARCHES ON!

(Crenshaw uses a pencil as a flute, Cheato grabs the American flag from the stand behind the desk, and with Hobo and his wastebasket drum, they march around the office as if they were "The Spirit of 1776" All the others join the parade, singing with patriotic exuberance. All except Jessica and Jorden, who look on in horror.)

OTHER COMEDIANS. *(Full volume.)*

LORDY, HOW WE TRY TO FOOL YA
LORDY, HOW WE TRY TO FOOL YA
LORDY HOW WE TRY TO FOOL YA
OUR SPENDING MARCHES ON!

(They parade around the set, triumphantly, until....)

JESSICA. Stop it! Stop it right now!!!

(As she jumps up, the various clowns and comedians freeze.)

JESSICA. *(CONT'D)* Shame on you for making a mockery of this country! There are hundreds of millions of honest Americans who still believe in the principles this nation was founded on. Freedom. Dignity. Honor. Hard work. Personal integrity! Principles each of you scoff at with your deceitful actions!

JORDEN. Jessica, Remember your position!

JESSICA. I have, Jorden. But I also remembered I am a citizen of this country first, and an employee of this government second. *(With rising heat.)* I know most people would rather vote for a pretty face than a courageous soul. But that's going to change! We will clean up this government and get rid of every politician who is incompetent, greedy or corrupt! I'm tired of Watergates and Whitewaters, Travelgate, Trumpgates and Whatevergates. I'm sick of earmarks, backroom deals, pork-barrel projects and runaway spending!

CRENSHAW. *(Innocently.)* Does that mean she didn't like my speech?

(Jessica looks like she is going to explode. All those years of compromising her ideals have crystallized into this single moment. She has never felt so alive.)

JESSICA. No, sir. I did not! And I'm going to walk right into that press conference next door and blow the whistle on your dirty little scheme!

JORDEN. Jessica! You can't do that!

JESSICA. I have to, Jorden. Democracy isn't a spectator sport. I thought you, of all people, would finally wake up and see that it's time to stop letting all these clowns and crooks and con artists run our country! Now, if you all will excuse me, I have a statement to make.

(She turns toward the door, Stage Right.)

CRENSHAW. Gentlemen, I believe it would be in our best interests if we restrain Miss Woodard before she talks to the press.

(The mob of comics surround Jessica, force her out the Stage Left door.)

JORDEN. No! Leave her alone!

JESSICA. *(Offstage.)* Jorden! Help me! Help!!!

JORDEN. *(Trying to stop them.)* Stop it! Leave her alone! Jessica!

(Hobo bonks Jorden on the head with his wastebasket. He drags the unconscious Jorden downstage, and flings his body on the sofa, Unable to resist, Hobo swipes Jorden's wallet and dashes out after the others.)

BLACKOUT

ACT TWO
Scene 2

(With the stage still dark, a chorus of faraway voices drift in.)

OFFSTAGE VOICES. *(Singing)*

HAVE YOU HEARD
THE EXCITEMENT IS GROWING
SPREAD THE WORD
THERE'S A NEW WIND BLOWING
A NEW FACE IN TOWN
HISTORY IS MADE TODAY
THERE'S A CHANGE IN THE WHITE HOUSE
A NEW LEADER OF THE USA

AT RISE: Jorden is sprawled out on the sofa asleep, exactly as he was at the opening. Only this time he is muttering and thrashing about.

JORDEN. *(Mumbling. Eyes closed.)* ... no... leave her alone... you can't...

JESSICA. *(OFFSTAGE)* Jorden! Jorden!

JORDEN. Huh... Wha..?

(Jessica enters, exactly as she did in the beginning of Act I.)

JESSICA. Jorden! What are you doing?! The new President will be here any minute!

JORDEN. What...oh, I....uh, must have drifted off to sleep...

JESSICA. How can you sleep at a time like this?!

JORDEN. ... Jessica. I had the worst nightmare... We were in the White House, just like now... but all the politicians were clowns, crooks, or con artists... it was terrible!

JESSICA. We can discuss the psychological implications of your nightmare another time. Right now, we have to make sure everything is in place for the new President's arrival.

(She shakes her head at his grogginess, then starts to exit.)

JORDEN. Jessica, wait!

JESSICA. What now, Jorden?

(He crosses to her and kisses her passionately. It is a long, desperate, soulful kiss, ten years in the making. She does not resist. When he breaks it off, they stare into each other's eyes.)

JESSICA. *(CONT'D)* Okay. What was that for?

JORDEN. I've waited ten years to do that. I didn't want to let another moment slip by without letting you know how I feel.

JESSICA. Oh? And how exactly do you feel?

JORDEN. I love you, Jessica. I always have.

(She breaks away, turns casually back to him.)

JESSICA. You expect me to be surprised?

JORDEN. You knew?!

JESSICA. You're a terrific Chief of Protocol, Jorden Fletcher. However, you're not exactly subtle when it comes to hiding your feelings.

JORDEN. *(Rattled.)* So, I've heard.

JESSICA. What?

JORDEN. Nothing. Just a silly dream. *(Looks up at her.)* So where does this leave us, Jessica? Will we ever have a future together? Or do I have to follow you around Washington like a lovesick puppy for another decade or two?

JESSICA. Get a hold of yourself, Fletcher. We have a job to do.

(She sees the disappointment on his face.)

JESSICA. *(CONT'D)* We can discuss that kiss over dinner. I'll pick you up at eight.

JORDEN. Really?

JESSICA. Try to wear something a little less stuffy, okay?

JORDEN. *(Brightening.)* I can do that!

(She is about to exit, when Jorden calls to her.)

JORDEN. *(CONT'D)* Jessica. Sorry, one more thing…I know this may sound a little strange, but...who exactly are we waiting for?

JESSICA. President Trump, of course.

(She ducks out the door. Jorden, alone in the Oval Office, considers this for a moment. Then slowly, his eyes grow large, and he lets out a horrifying scream.)

JORDEN. Noooooo!

BLACKOUT

(Out of the darkness we hear Jorden scream…)

JORDEN. Wake me up! Wake me Uu-u-up!!!

CURTAIN FALLS

EPILOGUE

(The entire cast re-enters in front of the closed curtain.)

"CHANGE IN THE WHITE HOUSE" REFRAIN

FULL CAST. *(Singing.)*

OUR PLAY IS DONE
BUT WE'RE STILL NERVOUS
THOSE IN CHARGE
THEY BARELY SERVE US
LET'S DEMAND THE BEST
COME THE NEXT ELECTION DAY
MAKE A CHANGE FOR OUR COUNTRY
WITH NEW LEADERS FOR THE USA!

LET'S MAKE CHANGE FOR OUR COUNTRY
A CHANGE FOR OUR COUNTRY
A CHANGE FOR OUR COUNTRY
BETTER LEADERS FOR THE USA!

The End

from "A Day at the White House"

lyrics by Vin Morreale

music by Eric B. Sirota

♩ = 168 Drum pattern ♩ = 168

ppp *f*

♩ = 168 ♩ = 168 *pp*

G3 Fsus2/G G° G

pp

5

Have you heard? Spread the word. Have you heard, Spread the word.

G3 Fsus2/G G° G G3 Fsus2/G G° G

9

Have you heard, Spread the word. Have you heard, the ex-

f *f*

Fsus2/G G° G C C+

ff *f*

2
Song #1 - A Change In The White House
12
ff
f
F Gm7/F
cite-ment is grow - ing. Spread the word There's a new wind blow- ing. A new face in
Am/C C7/G F B♭/D B° Em/G C F Gm7/F

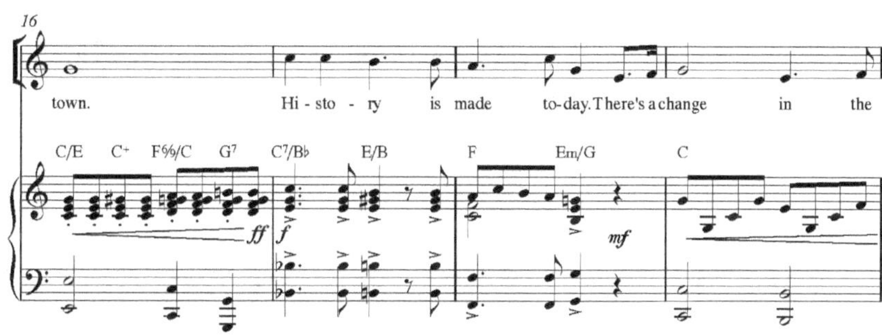
16
town. Hi - sto - ry is made to-day. There's a change in the
C/E C+ F6/9/C G7 C7/B♭ E/B F Em/G C
ff
f
mf

20
♩ = 168
White- house. A new lea - der of the U. S. A. He's the one who
C Em7/D E♭ F7/E♭ G7 C C C C+
f
ff
f

Song #1 - A Change In The White House
3
25
To - day is his in-au-gu-ra - tion.
charmed the na - tion. To-day is his in-au-gu-ra - tion. A new sense of hope.
Am/C C7/G F B♭/D B° Em/G G7 C F E♭ A♭7 A♭7sus4 A♭7♯4 A♭7
mf f
30
change in the White house.
Sure to be a bright er day. There's a change in the White - house. A new
D♭7/C♭ F/C F♯ Fm/A♭ D♭ Fm D♭ Fm
f mf f
34
lea - der of the U. S. A. He says he will
E F♯7/E A♭7 D♭ D D+
ff f
Song #1 - A Change In The White House 10/19/20
3

38
keep his pro - mi-ses. He'll show all the doubt - ing Tho-mas-es. The peo - ple have
Bm/D D7/A G C/E C#o F#m/A A Bb/D Bb

43
Democracy
De-mo-cra-cy
spo - ken. De - mo - cra - cy has had its say. There's a
/A A D F#/C# F# G F#m
ff
f

49
change in the White House. A new lea-der of the U. S. A.
D D/F# F G7/F A7 D
ff

53
He's just one more po - li - ti - cian. We'll re - port with sus-pi - sion.
Gm GmM7 Gm7 Gm6 Gm GmM7 Gm7 Gm6
mf

57
A quick ho - ney moon. A quick ho - ney - moon.
F♯ Bm/F♯ E Am/E

61
Then back to grid-lock each and eve-ery day. There's no change in the White-house. Onmore
C7/B♭ C E F Em/G C Em
ff f mf f

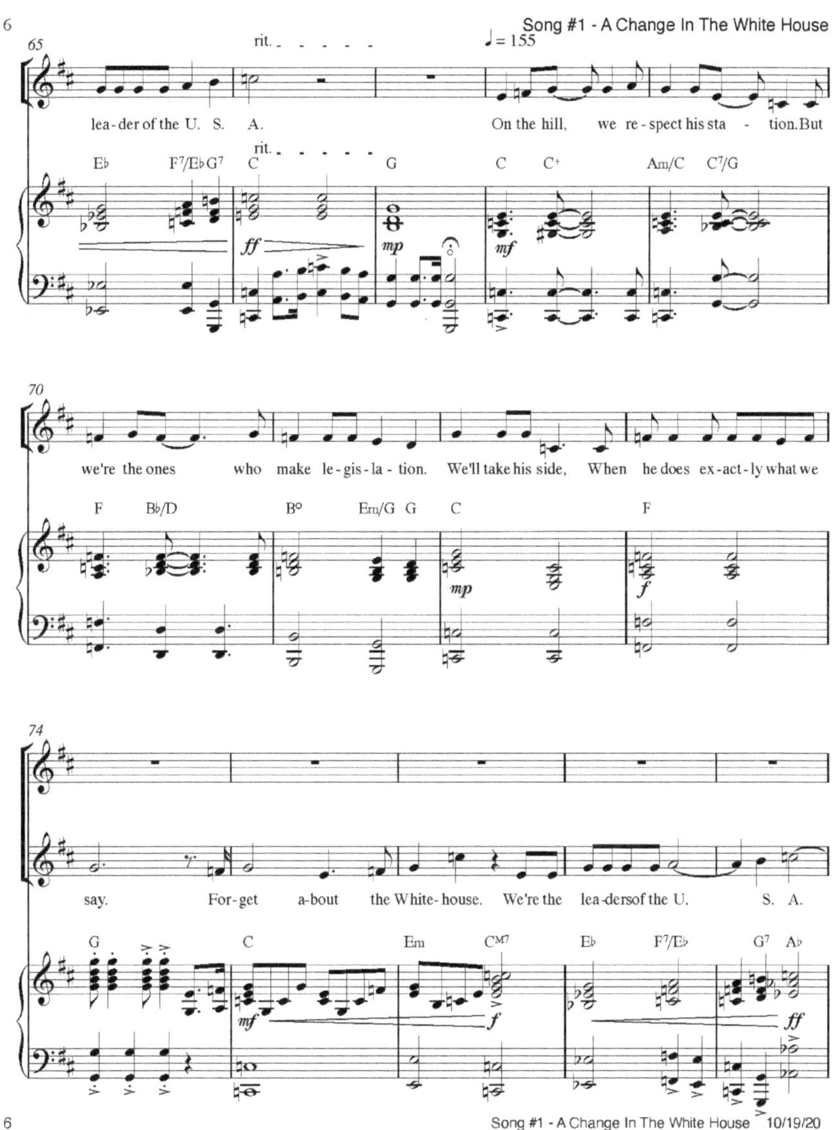
65
rit.
♩= 155
lea-der of the U. S. A.
On the hill, we re-spect his sta - tion. But
rit.
E♭ F7/E♭ G7 C G C C+ Am/C C7/G
ff
mp
mf
70
we're the ones who make le-gis-la-tion. We'll take his side, When he does ex-act-ly what we
F B♭/D B° Em/G G C F
mp
f
74
say. For-get a-bout the White-house. We're the lea-ders of the U. S. A.
G C Em CM7 E♭ F7/E♭ G7 A♭
mf
f
ff

79
rit.
♩= 120
A year from now we'll start to grum - ble. As his polls be-
G
C C+ Am/C C7/G F B♭/D
f mf mp

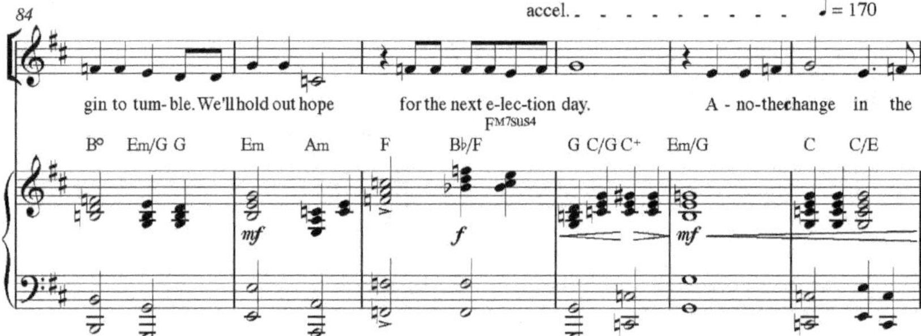
84
accel.
♩= 170
gin to tum- ble. We'll hold out hope for the next e-lec-tion day. A - no-the change in the
FM7sus4
B° Em/G G Em Am F B♭/F G C/G C+ Em/G C C/E
mf f mf

90

White House. With a new lea-der of the U. S. A.

Eb F7/Eb G7 Am Am/G# C/G C/F# FM7

96

We'll make a change in the White House. A change in the White House. A change in the

G7 C C/E Fm Db Db7/C F#m

ff mf rit.

102

White House. A new lea - der of the U. S. A.

D/C A7 A9 A7 A7sus4 A7 G7/F A7 D/A Bm7 D

= 170 rit. rit. ff

107

fff sfz

lyrics by Vin Morreale

This Is Where It Starts

from "A Day at the Whitehouse"

music by Eric B. Sirota

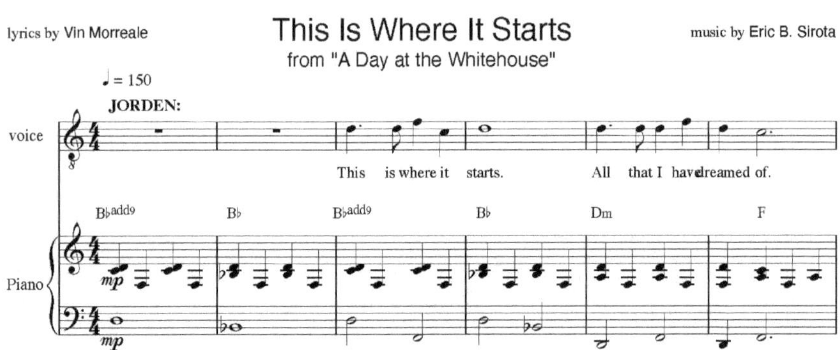

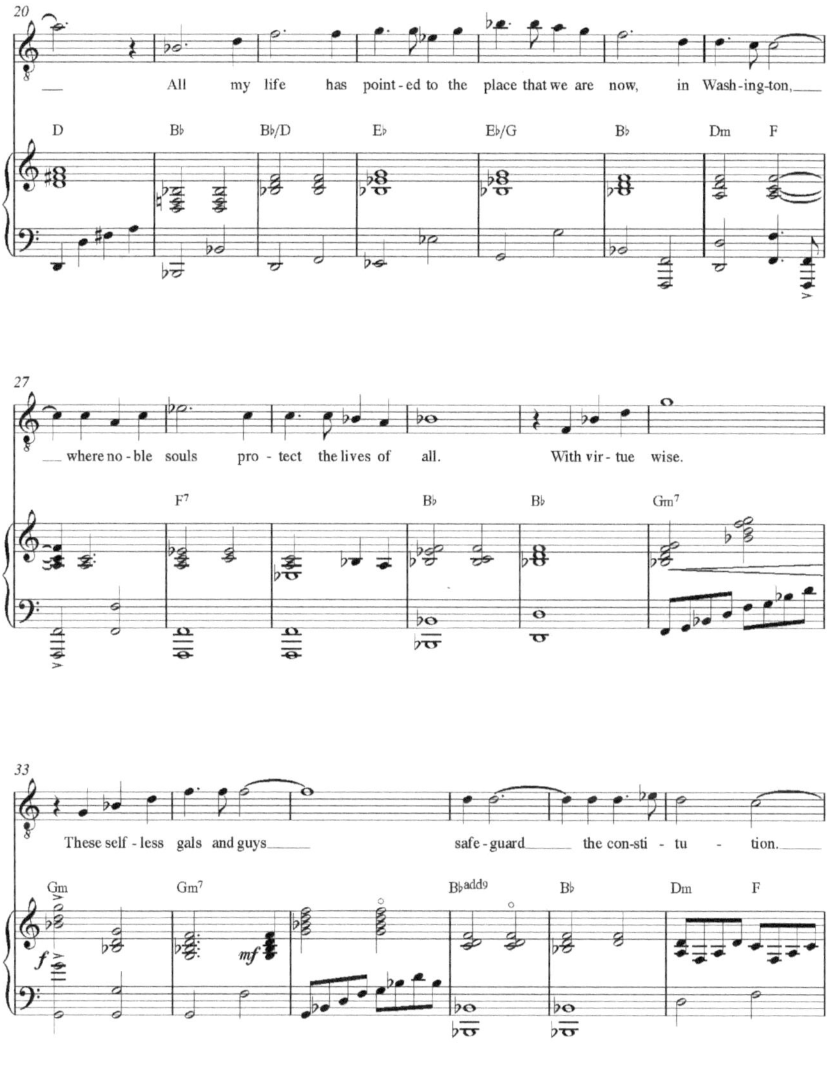

20

All my life has point-ed to the place that we are now, in Wash-ing-ton,

D Bb Bb/D Eb Eb/G Bb Dm F

27

where no-ble souls pro-tect the lives of all. With vir-tue wise.

F7 Bb Bb Gm7

39
And thanks to fate
I join this great and lof - ty in - sti -
Gm7
Dm
Gm
44
tu - tion.
All my life has point-ed to the place that we are
E♭ F F7/E♭ F7 B♭ B♭/D E♭ E♭/G
50
now, in Wash-ing-ton, where no-ble souls pro - tect the lives of all.
B♭ Dm F F7 B♭ B♭
mf
57
This is where it starts.
Ev - ery-thing I've worked for.
All that I be -
B♭sus2 B♭ Dm/F F B♭sus2

4
This Is Where It Starts
62
lieve, and now my choice is clear. A brand new pre - si - dent. A chance to make a
B♭ Dm B♭ Fsus4 F E♭ F Gm B♭ Dm
f ff
rit.
69
dif - ference. For post - e - ri - ty, and all that I hold dear.
F B♭ Dm F E♭ Dm B♭/D F7
fff
♩= 145
rit.
76
This is where it starts. I pray that I am worth - y. But with you by my side, my
B♭sus2 B♭ Dm Dm/F F Dm Gm E♭
f ff
♩= 117 ♩= 100
82
dreams will all come true. Shar ing them with you./Shar ing them with you, is
Cm F Dm B♭M7 B♭M7 B♭M7 Gm
mf mp
4 This Is Where It Starts 10/17/20

This Is Where It Starts
5
♩ = 120
87
rit.
all I want to do.
E♭ F7 E♭ F7 Fadd9 Cm9 B♭
mp

PIANO SCORE

lyrics by Vin Morreale
Song #3 - Obfuscation
music by Eric B. Sirota
from "A Day at the Whitehouse"
♩ = 155
CRENSHAW:
A lit-tle po-li-tics. A bit of that and this. A
G
D
G
G
Piano
lit - tle slight of hand to co - ver what's a- miss. Cue the smoke and mir- rors.
D
G
G
Flash the shi - ny lights. Be - fore they know what hit 'em you can take a - way their rights.
D
G

2
Song #3 - Obfuscation
It's all an il - lu - sion, a ma-gic trick, you see. But if you see, it's up to me to con
fuse you to - tal - ly. Obs-fu - ca - tion! Con-ster - na - tion. It
all comes down to this. De-di - ca- tion, to Pre - va - ri - ca - tion. Their words are mean-ing - less All their
words are mean-ing- less.
CHEATO:
A lit-tle jing-o - is - m A sound-bite to re - peat.
2
Song #3 - Obfuscation 10/17/20

Song #3 - Obfuscation
3
If you say just what you mean, they'll know that you're a cheat. Dance a-round the is-sues.
G C C
Mud-dy up the facts. And if you're caught the best de-fense is an un-pro-voked at-tack.
G C
CRENSHAW & CHEATO:
Obs-fu-ca -tion! Con-ster-na -tion. It all comes down to this. De-di-
G C Am C Am C G7 C
ca-tion to Pre-va-ri-ca - tion. Their words are mean-ing-less All their words are mean-ing-less.
Am C Am C G7 C G7 C

41
Con - si - der it a pri- mer, on po - li - ti - cal de - ceit.
C
44
Ly - ing has its own re - wards.The ho - nest know de - feat. Let the ho - nest know de - feat!
G C G C

Song #4 -What Would George Washington Think?

lyrics by Vin Morreale | from "A Day at the Whitehouse" | music by Eric B. Sirota

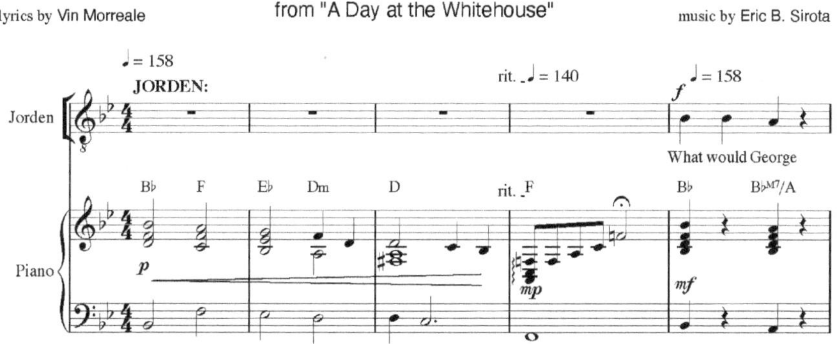

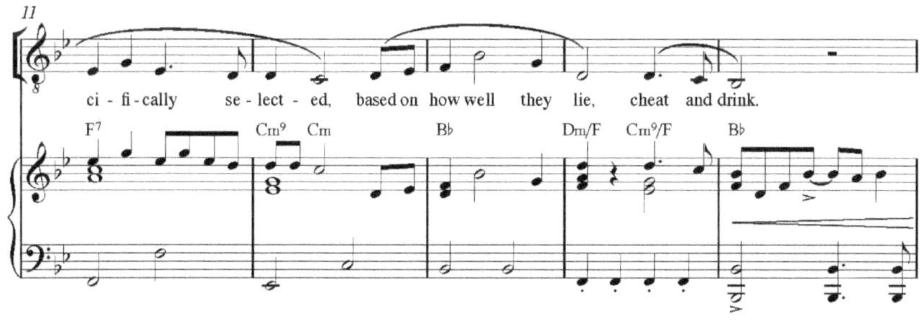

2

16
f
Now what would ho - nest
B♭7/A♭
G
G7
C
CM7/B
ff
f

20
Abe say? Of our gov-ern-ment gone so far a-stray. There's a class of no - bi-li-ty. We
Am7
C
Am
Am7/G
FM7
Bø7
E
Dm

25
re - e - lect till se - ni - li - ty, with the po-wer to raise their own pay.
G7
Dm9/F
Dm
C
Em/G
Dm9/G
F9
G
G9
G7

Song #4 -What Would George Washington Think?
3
JESSICA:
Oh, those dreams and be - liefs that they fought for, in those
JORDEN:
Oh, those dreams and be - liefs that they fought for, in those
C G F Em E C Am Em
days of re - bel - lion and strife.
Their lof - ty i-
Am C/E Dm9 Dm D7sus4/G D7sus4/G C G
de- als, de - ter-mi - na-tion of steel,
forged the Am - e ri - can
F D7sus4 Dm7 F/A Am/C C7/B♭ C/E C7/B♭ F E Am C/G

4
Song #4 -What Would George Washington Think?
47
rit.
way of life. The Am e - ri - can way
way of life. The Am
G9 Dm G G7/F E C/G Csus4/G G7
ff
mf
52
the Am - e ri - can way of life.
e ri - can way the Am - e ri - can way of life.
C/G G9 Dm C/G G9 Dm C G F Em
58
JESSICA:
♩= 158
Could Jef - fer-son do an - y - thing but laugh? At each cur-rent mis-state-
E G C CM7/B Am7 C Am Am7/G
mp
mf
4
Song #4 -What Would George Washington Think? 10/10/20

Song #4 -What Would George Washington Think?
5
65
ment and gaffe. Would he spin in his grave at the vi-sion he gave. Now
FM7
E
Dm
G7
E
f
mf
68
JESSICA:
filled with cor - rup-tion and graft? Oh, those dreams and be -
JORDEN:
Oh, those dreams and be -
C
Em/G
G
F9
G
G9
G7
C
G
F
Em
f
74
liefs that they fought for, in those days of re - bel - lion and
liefs that they fought for, in those days of re - bel - lion and
E
C
Am
Em
Am
C/E
Dm9
Dm
Song #4 -What Would George Washington Think? 10/10/20
5

6
Song #4 -What Would George Washington Think?
79
strife. Our faith in the spine - less bureau -ro - cra-cy
strife. Our faith in the spine less bureau - ro - cra-cy
D7sus4/G D7sus4/G C G F D7sus4 Dm7 F/A Am/C
84
mind- less. To bank-rupt the A -me - ri - can way of life.
mind- less. To bank-rupt the A -me ri - can way of life.
C7/B♭ C/E C7/B♭ F E Am C/G G9 Dm G G7/F
ff
90
The Am e - ri - can way the Am
The Am -e ri - can way the Am
E C/G Csus4/G G7 C/G G9 Dm
mf
6
Song #4 -What Would George Washington Think? 10/10/20

Song #4 - What Would George Washington Think?
7
e ri - can way of life.
Is there
C/G G9 Dm C G F Em E G7
101
rit.
any-thing brave men could say
Af ter two hund-red years of de- cay?
Yet, with each ad-mi-ni-
C CM7/B Am7 C Am Am7/G FM7 Bø7 E Em
106
stra - tion, we hope for sal - va-tion. And for some-one to show us the way.
Dm G7 DmM9 C F/C Em/G G C rit.
Song #4 - What Would George Washington Think? 10/10/20
7

112
♩= 140
Just some - one to show
Just some - one to show
G7 C F/C F C Em/G
116
us the way.
us the way.
G G9 C G F Em E

PIANO SCORE

Song #5 - More Than the Sum of Her Parts

lyrics by Vin Morreale

from "A Day at the Whitehouse"

music by Eric B. Sirota

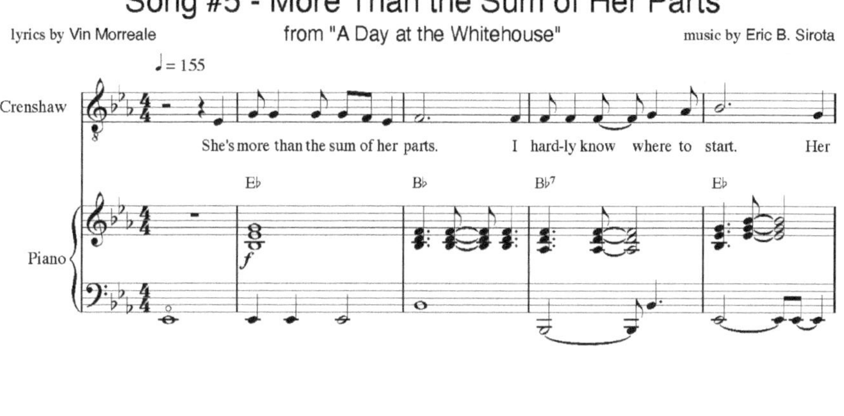

2
Song #5 - More Than the Sum of Her Parts
14
wo-man like that. Can lay a guy flat. She's more than the sum of her parts. She's a
E♭7 A♭ B♭7 E♭ Cm E♭ B♭7
18
♩= 171
Partly speaking
hot - tie with a bo - dy that's not ea - si - ly ig-nored. Her de - mean-or is ob-scen- er. Once you've
E♭ E♭+ Cm E♭+ E♭ B♭ B♭7
21
rit.
♩= 145
scene her, Oh, my lord! She's a la - dy slight-ly sha - dy, by the way she makes me feel. Is all
B♭7 E♭ A♭ Fm A♭7 A♭ G♭
24
♩= 160
♩= 135
squig- gly, slight-ly gig- gly, when she's wrig- gly, it's un- real! She's more than the sum of her
F G♭ F°/A♭ F7 G7 C
pp
f
2
Song #5 - More Than the Sum of Her Parts 10/17/20

28
parts. Built to man - hand - le men's hearts. Let me be spe - ci - fic. Her
G
G7
C
C7
F

32
breasts are ter - ri - fic! She's more than the sum of her parts. Though I ad - mit I'm a big fan of her
G7
C
F
Dm
C
F

♩= 160
36
rit.
parts. She's more than the sum of her parts.
rit.
C
G7
C
sfz
fff

Climes They Are A Changin
lyrics by Vin Morreale
from "A Day at the Whitehouse"
music by Eric B. Sirota
♩ = 155
♩ = 155
CRENSHAW:
voice
Piano
In the o - cean, I've a no - tion,
that it's get - ting hot - ter
Ca - li - forn - ia Let me warn ya. We're
run-ning out of wa ter.
Mis - sis - sip - pi
Is more drip - py. Ri-vers will be ri - sin'.
Dat pol-lu tion ain't no so-lu - tion.

JESSICA & JORDEN:
Dat I am sur - mis- sin'.
Feel the heat.
C G G C G C F
In the street. Tem-pera - tures are soar - ing.
Da north pole. No long - er col'
C F Am C F G F C
Po - lar bear is roar - ing.
CRENSHAW:
Green-house smok-in' has us chok-'in
F G C G C/G F C G
I'm not jo-'kin The pla-net's bro-ken.
All a-bout the
F C G C C C

Climes They Are A Changin
3
37
peo - ple doubt. Ex - perts lec - ture pure con - jec - ture. They ex - pect your
G C/G C
41
rit.
times run out. Lis - ten how they rant and shout. O' the climes they are a' chang - in'
F G G G G Em G C
46 ♩ = 155
Fear da warm - in' In - creased storm - in'. They say the end is
C F C F Am C
50
near___ Who will pros - per from de phos - pher in our at - mo - sphere___.
F G F C F G C
Climes They Are A Changin 10/18/20
3

4
Climes They Are A Changin
55
ALL:
Glo - bal warm - in' is trans-from - in'__ our en - vir - on-
C F C F Am C
59
ment; yeah. Noth - in' to__ it? Did we do__ it? Dat's de arg - u - ment; yeah.
F G F C F G C
64
Green-house smok-in' has us cho-k'in I'm not jo-'kin The pla-net's bro-ken.
C/G F C G F C G C C
69
CRENSHAW:
Arc - tic heat - in' Ice re-trea 'tin Pen guins chase a melt ing
C F C F Am

73
gla - cier. Just in case ya 'atten - tion's fleet-ing the
C/G G C F C F

76
rit.
rit.
3
pre - si-dent will hold a meet - ing cause the climes they are a' chang - in'
Am G C G Em G C
Ped. Ped.

PIANO SCORE

Song #6a - Climes They Are a Changin' Reprise

lyrics by Vin Morreale

from "A Day at the Whitehouse"

music by Eric B. Sirota

♩ = 145

CRENSHAW:

I'll preach the to - pic, like I'm a pro - phet,

C C F C F

Piano

f

PIANO SCORE

lyrics by Vin Morreale

This Is Where It Ends
from "A Day at the Whitehouse"

music by Eric B. Sirota

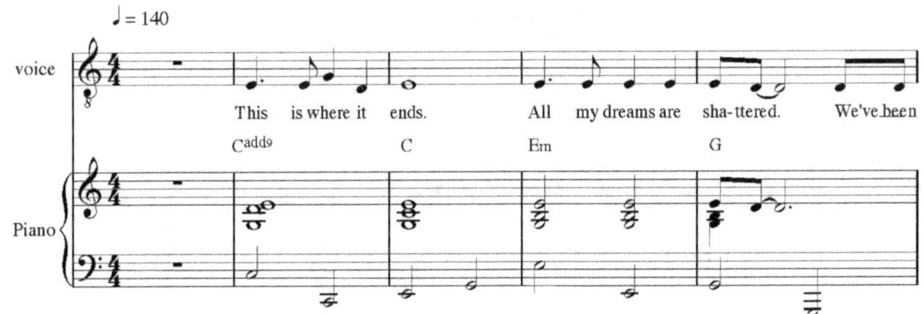

2
This Is Where It Ends
18
This is where it ends. I -deals - no long-er mat-ter. No - bi - li-ty's a
G Cadd9 C Em G C
24
joke. When crooks and fools a - bound. This is where it ends. The U. S. A. in
B7 Em G7 C Em FM7
30
ta - tters. When we e - lect a clown. When
C Bm
G7
34 Bm/D D7 G
we e - lect a clown.

PIANO SCORE

SONG #8 - Life of a Politician

lyrics by Vin Morreale

from "A Day at the Whitehouse"

music by Eric B. Sirota

♩=76

CRENSHAW:

Oh, the life of the po li - ti - cian is the life for me. Where

G G D

Piano

2
SONG #8 - Life of a Politician
7
spin doc-tors to co-ver when we act like jerks. We get free hair-cuts, me-als, and e-ven pos-tage too. Then
G B B G Am G
Ped.
9
make our selves ex-empt from laws we pass for you. We make our-selves ex-empt from laws we pass for you. Yes, the
A7 D7 G
11
JESSICA & JORDEN:
life of the po-li-ti-cian is the life for me. Cause I'd ra-ther have the mo-ney than my dig-ni-ty. He'd
C G C
13
CRENSHAW:
ra-ther have his mo-ney than his dig-ni-ty. There are
G C G

SONG #8 - Life of a Politician
3
scan- dals, deals and kick- backs, and lots of po-wer grabs. We can al-ways count on vo-ters to pick up the tabs. I've a-
C Cm Gsus4 G Dm C♯+ F
ssis- tants, pa ges, lob-by-ists and a staff of twelve. Who glad ly do the work while I en rich my- self. They'll
C Cm Gsus4 G D7 G
glad-ly do the work, while he en rich-es self. Yes, the life of the po-li - ti - cian is the life for me. And I
D7 G G D
know you'll re - e - lect us fore - ter - ni - ty. But you're on-ly get-ting ev ery-thing that you de serve. 'Cause
F D G D G D
SONG #8 - Life of a Politician 10/18/20
3

4
SONG #8 - Life of a Politician
some-how you for got that we were meant to serve. Some-how you for got that you're sup-posed to serve.
Oh, the life of the po-li - ti - cian is the life for me. Cause I'd
rit.
♩=74
ra ther have my mo-ney than my dig - ni - ty. Yes, the life of the po li - ti - cian is for me.'cause I'd
JESSICA & JORDEN:
ra-ther have my mo-ney than my dig - ni - ty. He'd ra-ther have his mo-ney than his dig -ni ty.
4
SONG #8 - Life of a Politician 10/18/20

PIANO SCORE

Song #9 - I'm in Love With My PC

lyrics by Vin Morreale

from "A Day at the Whitehouse"

music by Eric B. Sirota

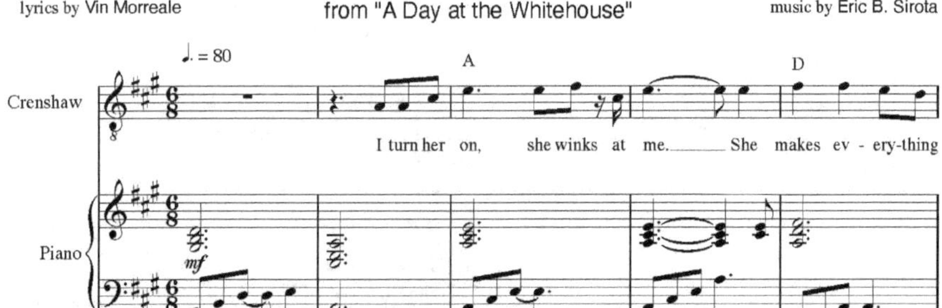

2
Song #9 - I'm in Love With My PC
16
A C♯m G♯° A A
love's noth-ing ob - scene. She's just pro grammed to be sex - y. I'm in love with my P
21
C♯m D E A C♯m G♯°
C, my com - pu - ter like no o - ther. I can in - put when I please, know-ing she won't out - put for a-
27
♩ = 220
A A E7 A
no- ther. She knows the Ti-gres and Eu - phra - tes. Can tell cou-pons from Ku - wai - tis. What do I
33
♩ = 200
A D A D A E D A E7
need with oth - er la - dies. She's my main frame can't you see. I'm in love with my P.
2

Song #9 - I'm in Love With My PC
3
♩ = 200
A D A D A
C. She ne-ver calls my da-ta base I can al-ways speak her lang-uage. Al-
D A C#m C#m E7 G
though she does n't have a face, In her spread-sheet I can lang- guish. She's the Ap-ple of my
D F C G F A7
eye. The flash in my hard drive. I gig-gle when she Goog-les and dream of stream-ing
♩. = 70 ♩. = 80
D
live. I'm in love with my P C, my com-pu-ter like no o-ther. I can in-put when I
A D A
Song #9 - I'm in Love With My PC 10/18/20
3

4
Song #9 - I'm in Love With My PC
♩= 160
63
please, know-ing she won't out-put for a - no - ther. So what if I don't know RAM from ROM? Can
C♯m G♯o A D A
68
D A E A D A D A E
ne-ver take her to the PROM? I al-ways know where she's com-ing from. She boots up just for me.
74
D A E7 A ♩.= 70 B♭ ♩.= 80
I'm in love with my P C. They say soft - ware's ne-ver sen - su- al. Let them
79
E♭ B♭ Dm A°
talk I won't list - en. Till they've hand - led her per - if - erals. And seen how her hard-ware

Song #9 - I'm in Love With My PC
5
84
B♭
glist - ens. So I hope that you don't mind my tale of love ro - bo - tic. Some-times
E♭
F
89
Dm
A°
love's not on-ly blind. In my case, It's psy - cho-tic. I'm in love with my P C, my com
95
pu - ter like no o - ther. I can in - put when I please, know-ing she won't out-put for a-
♩ = 165
100
F7
no-ther. She knows the Ti-gres and Eu - phra-tes. Can tell cou-pons from Ku - wai-tis. What do I
Song #9 - I'm in Love With My PC 10/18/20
5

6 Song #9 - I'm in Love With My PC

PIANO SCORE

Song #10 - Love At First Grope
from "A Day at the Whitehouse"
lyrics by Vin Morreale
music by Eric B. Sirota
♩ = 140
MAE WAIST:
Can I have your ear mis - ter Pre-si-dent. Your cute lit-tle ear mis-ter
Pre-si-dent. It's so hard not to nib-ble and coo. Please
CRENSHAW: MAE WAIST:
do. Don't try to re - sist mis ter
Pre-si-dent. This lob-by-ist has ne-ver benn kissed. mis-ter Pre-si-dent. Well that might be slight-ly un -
true.
CRENSHAW:
You're the on - ly wo - man in this room for me; the love of my life at least 'til
Piano
C9 C C9 C Am7 Dm7 G7 CM7 C CM7 Dm7 G7 C Dm7 C C CM7 Em F
Copyright © 2016 Vin Morreale & Eric B. Sirota 6/30/20

2
Song #10 - Love At First Grope
MAE WAIST:
CRENSHAW:
MAE WAIST:
ten af - ter three. You're the one who sparks my de - sire.
Must be my looks.
Just your sig-na-ture
I re - quire.
Love at first grope.
How el - li - cit - ly fun!
You're the
third man this week I've told he's the on - ly one.
CRENSHAW:
Love at first grope.
So love-ly so pure.
Well I'm
not so sure a-bout pure. But when you throw me those curves I can hard-ly de - mur.
MAE WAIST:
Love at first grope.
It takes a

Song #10 - Love At First Grope
3
BOTH:
spe-cial man to make me feel this way; but luck-y for you he's out of town to - day. Love at first
Am7 D7 Am7 D F#7
♩= 90
grope. So ex ci-ting and new. You scam-ming me, while I'm con ning you. Love at first
BM7 G#m7 BM7 G#m7 C#m7 F#7 BM7 G#m7
rit.
grope. So what if it's not real. I ac - cept your of - fer,
BM7 G#m7 C#m7 C#m6 F#7
now close the deal.
BM7 B6 BM7 B
Song #10 - Love At First Grope 6/30/20
3

PIANO SCORE

Song #11 - Who Could Have Known (Questions)

lyrics by Vin Morreale from "A Day at the Whitehouse" music by Eric B. Sirota

2
Song #11 - Who Could Have Known (Questions)
15
dan - cers, who would fol-low the moves of a man. But some-how it changed. When, I can't
Am D Gsus4 G C C C+
20
say. I let some-one in. Then some-one went a - way. Why did-n't I know, how it would
Am C7 CM7 Am Fm D♭ Dm Dm
25
be? Was I so blind? Why could-n't I see? There's a cruel - i - ty in-he-rent in ques-tions. A
B♭ E+ Am G7 C
30
ra - zor dis-guised in the doubt. The worst part a-bout in-tro-spec-tion, is the an-swers you won't slip
F Dm Gsus4 G E Am D Dsus4 D
2

35
out. Now what can I do? Where can I go? Who can I trust? How will I
Gsus4 G C C+ Am C7 CM7 E
40
know? I was the per-son who had all the an-swers. The wo-man al-ways in con
Asus4 Am Am F Em G
44
trol. I laughed at the "leave-it-to chanc-ers" Tried to pre-tend I was whole. But
C E Am Dm G
49
some-how it changed. When, I can't say. I let some-one in. Then some-one went a-way.
C C+ Am C7 CM7 Am Fm Dm

54

How will it be? When I de-cide to fi-nal-ly let out all I'm hold-ing in-side. I

C+ Am D G E Am

PIANO SCORE

Song #12 - Regulation

lyrics by Vin Morreale

music by Eric B. Sirota

from "A Day at the Whitehouse"

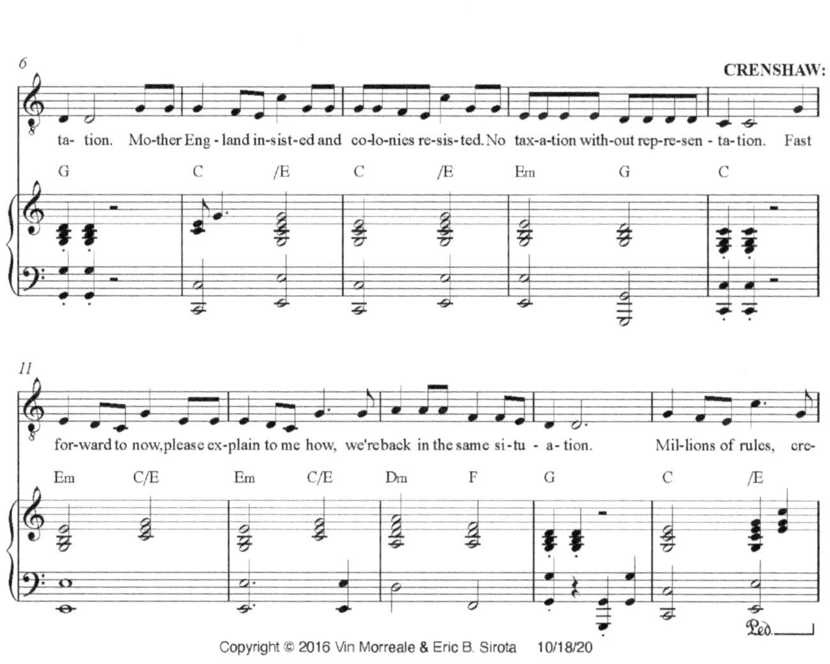

2
Song #12 - Regulation
16
BOTH:
a-ted by fools. Re-gu-la-tion is not le-gis - la-tion! Re-gu - la - tion; Please do what they say. Re-gu -
C /E /G Em G C Am/C C Am/C C
21
la - tion! Or we'll put you a-way. It's the law of the land by de-cree.
Am/C C Am/C C Dm Am G Dm Am
ff
26
Re-gu - la - tion! Yet you have no choice. Re-gu - la - tion! Not
G Am/C C Am/C C Am/C C
f
30
e-ven a voice. We as-sume that's how it should be. This per-ver sion of de-moc-ra-cy. A bu-rea-
Am/C C Dm Am G F Am G
2
Song #12 - Regulation 10/18/20

Song #12 - Regulation
3
34
crat's wet dream, you'll see. Re-gu - la - tion; Got us by the bills. Re-gu -
C G A Bm/D D Bm/D D
38
la - tion! They're ex - ert-ing their will. O-ver ev - ery part of our day.
Bm/D D Bm/D D Em Bm A C♯m/E
ff
42
Re-gu - la - tion! Some bu-rea-crat troll. Re-gu - la - tion! Has
A B7 C♯m/E E C♯m/E E C♯m/E E
sfz
f
46
ta-ken-con-trol. And now has the ul - ti mate say, on what you eat drive or pay. But
C♯m/E E F♯m C♯m B A C♯m B

50
how did it end up this way? Re-gu - la-tion in-stead of le-gis - la - tion.
E B C Em G C

PIANO SCORE
Song #13 - Truth is a Fungible Thing
lyrics by Vin Morreale
from "A Day at the Whitehouse"
music by Eric B. Sirota
♩. = 100
Crenshaw
Piano
Truth is a fun-gi-ble thing. Trust me, I know what I sing._ Just
yell, "It's fake news!" Then they'll change their views. Truth is a fun-gi-ble thing. Facts are a mes-sy af
fair. So I pull_them out of thin air. It helps to con-fuse. Claim you win when you lose.
rit.
♩. = 90
Facts are a mes-sy af - fair. What's a lit-tle white lie? Or Tweet well placed. If it keeps vo-ters still on your team?

2
Song #13 - Truth is a Fungible Thing
♩. = 100 A tempo
D DM7 C♯m E Bm E7 A E E7 A
Pro-mise-s made are so of-ten de- layed. Just learn not to say what you mean.
A tempo
A Bm E7 C♯m
Truth is a pli-a-ble thing. More like a bun-gie cord spring. Don't fret or re -gret. It's more
♩. = 85
accel.
F♯m Bm A E A E7 B
fun when you stretch it. That's why dis-in-fo-ma-tion is king. Ho-nes-ty's a re-la-tive
♩. = 100
C♯m F♯7 D♯m G♯m C♯m
thing. With an of-ten non-sen-si-cal ring. Some times in-de-fen-si-ble. Or in-com-pre hen-si-ble.
f
2
Song #13 - Truth is a Fungible Thing 10/18/20

Song #13 - Truth is a Fungible Thing
♩. = 100
3
Ho-nes-ty's a re-la-tive thing. Truth has a malle-a-ble side. I don't e-ven know when I
lied. A false-hood for-give-a-able make's life more liv-a-ble Truth has a malle-a-ble side. What's a
rit. slower
slower
lit-tle white lie? Or Tweet well placed. If it keeps vo-ters still on your team? Pro-mise s made are so
rit.
of-ten de-layed. Just learn not to say what you mean. I ne-ver say what I mean.
rit.
sfz

PIANO SCORE

Song #14 - More Than the Sum of His Parts

lyrics by Vin Morreale from "A Day at the Whitehouse" music by Eric B. Sirota

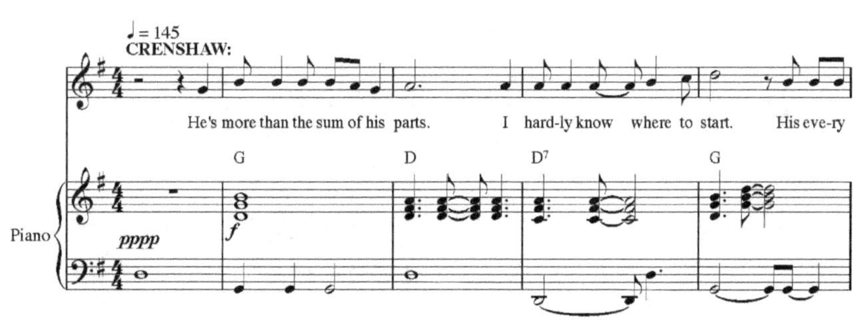

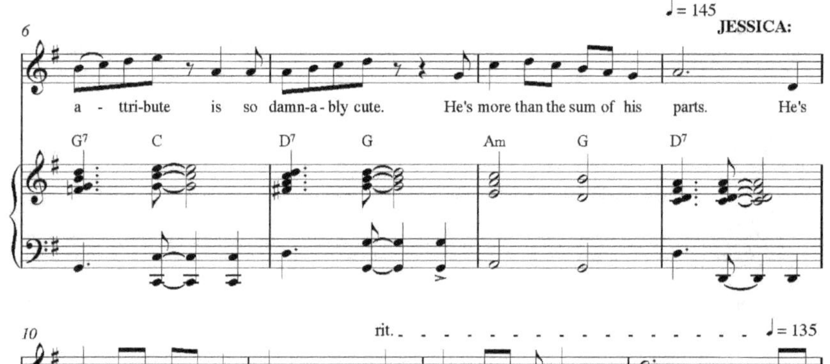

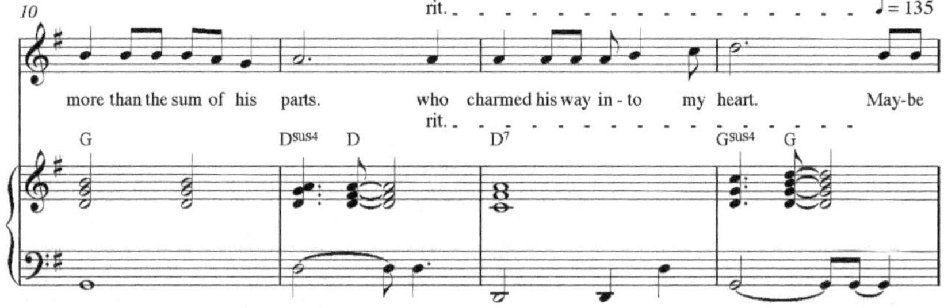

14
I should ex - plore,
how much I
a- dore.
He's more than the sum of his
parts.
G7
C
D7
G
Em
G
D7

18
rit.
So much more
than the
sum
of
his
parts.
A7
G
A7
D

Song #15 - Lordy, Lordy

lyrics by Vin Morreale

from "A Day at the White House"

music by arr. Eric B. Sirota

2
14
Piano Score
Song #15 - Lordy, Lordy
Lord' - y how we try and fool ya. The bud - get mar-ches on.
C C+ Am/E C7omit5 FM7 G6/D C C Dm7/G D7sus4/G Gsus4 G C C/G G C Ab+ Am Ab+

19
Mine eyes have seen the rap - ing of our poor e-co - no- my. With the
C Ab+ Am B° G C Ab+ Am Ab+ C/E Ab+ Am Ab+
Ped.

23
laws and re - gu-la - tions paid by you, and not by me. Yet we know we won't be blamed be-cause of
F F#° Fsus2/G F#° G G° G G7 C Ab+ Am/E C7omit5
2
Song #15 - Lordy, Lordy 10/8/20

26
vo - ter a - pa - thy. Our spend - ing march - es on. Lord' - y how we try and
FM7 G6/D C/E C Dm7G D7sus4/G Gsus4 G C C/G G C/G C+ Am Cb13/G
3

30
fool ya. Lord' - y how we try and fool ya. Lord' - y how we try and
C C+ Am/E E+ F Fb9 Fsus2/C F#o/B# G Go Eo/G G6 C C+ Am/E C7omit5

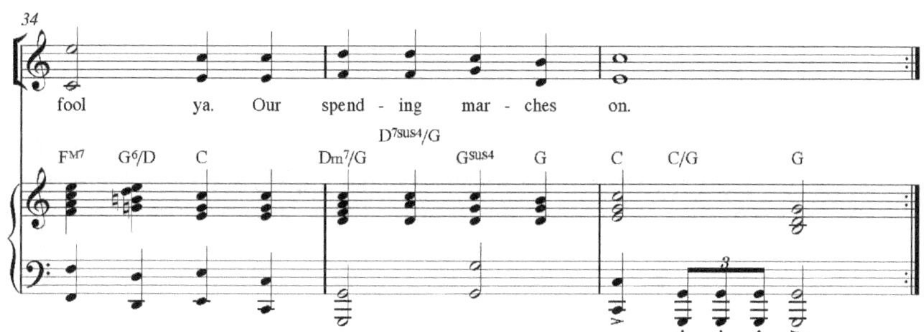
34
fool ya. Our spend - ing mar - ches on.
D7sus4/G
FM7 G6/D C Dm7/G Gsus4 G C C/G G
3

Song #14 - Ending
from "A Day at the White House"
lyrics by Vin Morreale
music by Eric B. Sirota
♩= 168
G3 Fsus2/G G° G G3 Fsus2/G G° G
pp
5
G3 Fsus2/G G° G Fsus2/G
8
G° G C C+ Am/C C7/G F Bb/D
ff f
Have you heard, the ex - cite-ment is grow - ing Spread the word There's a
Copyright © 2016 Vin Morreale & Eric B. Sirota 10/19/20

12
F Gm7/F
new wind blow - ing. A new face in town. Hi - sto - ry is
B° Em/G C F Gm7/F C/E C+ F6/9/C G7 C7/B♭ E/B
ff
f

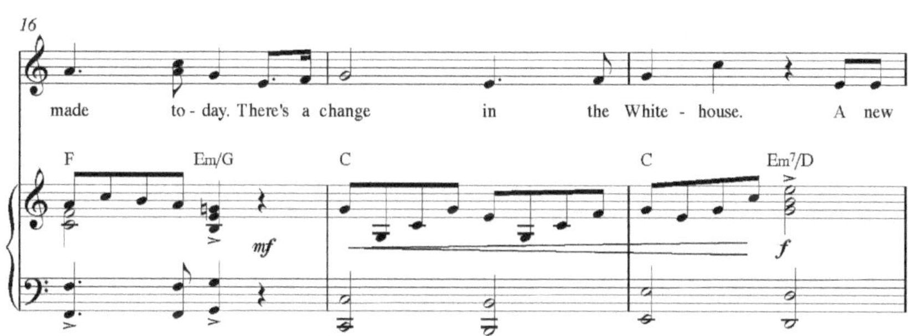
16
made to - day. There's a change in the White - house. A new
F Em/G C C Em7/D
mf
f

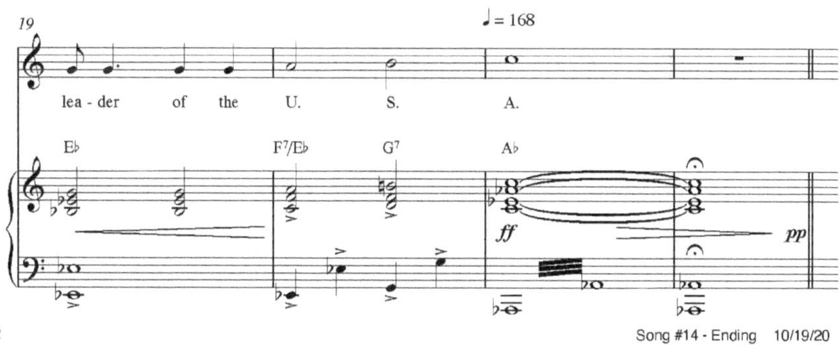
19
♩ = 168
lea - der of the U. S. A.
E♭ F7/E♭ G7 A♭
ff
pp

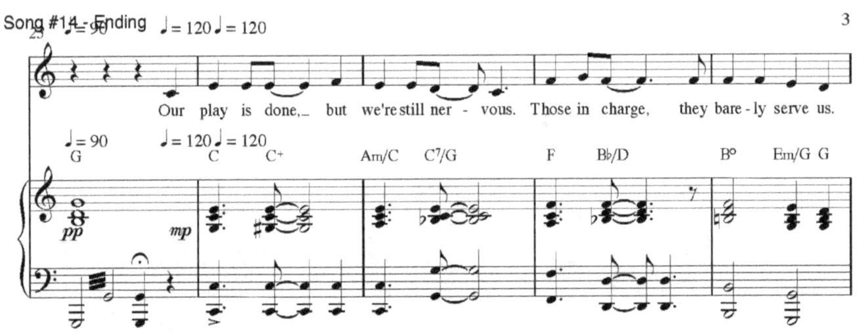
Song #14 - Ending
♩= 90
♩= 120 ♩= 120
3
Our play is done,_ but we're still ner - vous. Those in charge, they bare - ly serve us.
G C C+ Am/C C7/G F B♭/D B° Em/G G
pp
mp

28
accel.
♩= 168
Let's de-mand the best. come the next e-lec-tion day. Make a change for our coun-try. With
FM7sus4
Em Am F B♭/F G C/G C+ Em/G C C/E
mf
f
f
mf

34
new lea-ders for the U. S. A. Let's make a
E♭ F7/E♭ G7 Am Am/G♯ C/G C/F♯ FM7 G7
sfz
sfz
ffz
mf

4 Song #14 - Ending

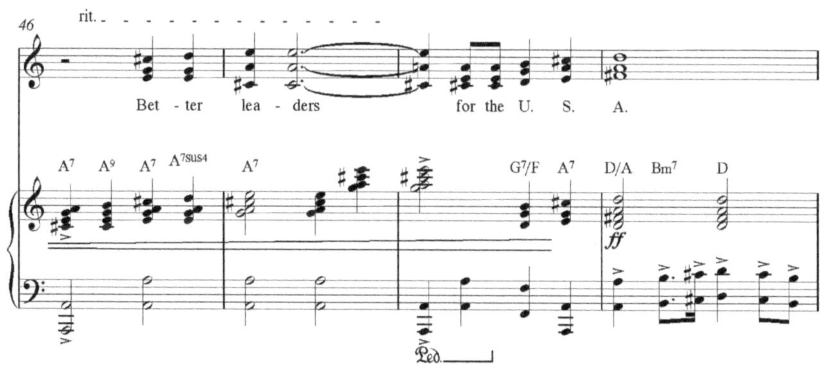

ORIGINAL CAST

CRENHAW SPARX	Beau Solley
JORDAN FLETCHER	Dwight Turner
JESSICA WOODARD	Sarah Turner Holland
CHEATO SPARX	Vin Morreale, Jr.
HOBO SPARX	Schwinn Hornblower
THE THREE STUPIDS	
BARRY	Beau Solley
BO	Rick Bucy
CURBEY	Stephen Preston
CABOT & ODDFELLOW	
JUDD CABOT	Gary Crockett
LOU ODDFELLOW	Will Adams
MAE WAIST	Barbara Polk
W.Z. FIELDING	Randy Davidson
CHORUS	Chauncey E. Arnold
	Amber Hurst
	Gary Crockett
	Sarah Turner Holland

Composer/Accompanist	Eric B. Sirota
Producer	Mandy Michelle Morreale
Director	Vin Morreale, Jr.
Music Directors	Kim Abele
	Fred Bogert
Music Producers	Fred Bogert
	JD Miller

About The Composer

Eric B. Sirota is a composer, playwright and physicist.

He studied music composition at Brown University and received his PhD in Physics at Harvard.

His first work performed in NYC was as composer on a 15-minute version of "A Day at the Whitehouse", where he met playwright, Vin Morreale Jr., as part of the West Village Musical Theatre Festival in 2012.

Since then, Eric's musical, "Frankenstein," based on Mary Shelley's novel, has been playing Off-Broadway at St. Luke's Theatre for almost 3 years. "Your Name on My Lips", a musical about following one's passion with obsession and commitment, was produced by Theater for the New City .

He is currently developing "Go, My Child", a musical about leaving one's parents, infertility and the search for truth, set against a background of xenophobia - an original account of the early lives of familiar biblical characters. And his newest musical, "A Good Day" is about the power of music to rekindle memory and awaken the mind.

ABOUT THE PLAYWRIGHT

Vin Morreale, Jr. is an internationally produced playwright, published author and award-winning screenwriter.

Vin was a founding member of the San Francisco Playwrights Center, the Highview Arts Center and the Senseless Bickering Comedy Theatre. He has directed hundreds of works for stage, screen and radio across the country. He was awarded the prestigious *Al Smith Writing Fellowship*, and his scripts, stage plays, documentaries, museum exhibits and radio comedy have received hundreds of productions around the world, as well as being translated into Chinese, Italian, Russian and Spanish.

Vin has sold material to network and cable television networks, had screenplays optioned and produced, and his work has been seen in more than 15 countries. He was named a top screenwriter by both The International Screenwriters Association and TheBlacklist.org, and was one of the first inductees in the Kentucky Film & TV Hall of Fame.

As president of *Vin Morreale Casting,* along with his nationally known *Burning Up The Stage* acting workshops, he has helped nearly 30,000 actors find work in movies, TV, stage and video.

Also by Vin Morreale, Jr.

ACADEMY ARTS PRESS

http://academyartspress.com/shop-for-books

The KISS ME Curse
The Carrie Variations
300 Monologues
Two Character Chaos
150 Acting Scenes
Chicken Fat For The Damaged Psyche
Knowing When To Leave
Dark Wilderness & Other Stories
Mabel The Maple
Too Many Rules

DRAMATIC PUBLISHING

dramaticpublishing.com/authors/profile/view/url/vin-morreale-jr

Burning Up The Stage – *Monologues & Audition Scenes for Actors from 6 to 70*
Breaking & Entering
House of The Seven Gables
Uncool
Nicky's Secret
Southern Discomfort
The Happy Holidays Collection

ELDRIDGE PUBLISHING

histage.com/search?q=Morreale

The Fairyland Detective Agency
Sonoma White & The Seven Dolts
Fairies, Fantasies & Just Plain Fun

OFF THE WALL PUBLISHING

offthewallplays.com

Captive Christmas
Forsaken
Exquisite Anxieties – Seven Slivers of Suspense
Temp Work
Empathy – A Celebration of Women's Voices
Ladies Guild Pre-Christmas Planning Session

CPSIA information can be obtained
at www.ICGtesting.com
Printed in the USA
LVHW081750021121
702257LV00016B/1213